CASSANDRA

Reflections in a Mirror

by

Robert Connor

with an Introduction by George Brown

CASSELL · LONDON

CASSELL & COMPANY LTD
35 Red Lion Square, London, WC1
Melbourne, Sydney, Toronto
Johannesburg, Auckland

First published 1969

S.B.N. 304 93341 4

© Robert Connor 1969

Printed in Great Britain by
The Camelot Press Ltd., London and Southampton
F.069

CONTENTS

INTRODUCTION

by George Brown

THE Big Men that have passed through one's life, coloured one's outlook and thereby influenced the pattern of one's subsequent development are inevitably very few. Bill Connor was one of my special privileges.

I liked him. But then so I have many folk. I respected him, whether or not I disagreed with him, which certainly narrows the field a bit. But this alone doesn't put him into the small circle of treasured friends in which he figures in my memories. Others, as does the author of this book, claim to detect some similarities in our make-up and nature. This, if true, would be flattering to me and could go part way to explaining my regard, since we all choose our heroes a little subjectively.

But I don't think that any or all of those things really satisfactorily and entirely explain the stature that he always seemed to me to have. For to me he really was a very big man. Genuine; always trying to be just; with an uncanny instinct for picking the phoney from the real. One could not help but admire his sincere humanity; the sheer breadth of his capacity—he could write on any topic, knowing intuitively whether to treat it seriously or with his innate sense of humour and sense of the ridiculous; the courage of his convictions blessed always with humility. It was things like these that made him really stand out head and shoulders above so many. And something else too. You never saw him claiming friendship with anyone whom one would not be proud to claim as one's own friend.

I cannot see anyone who knew Bill Connor reading this book, as I have, with anything but the pleasure it gave me. It tells familiar stories and unfamiliar ones. It glows with filial pride and yet still gives us a portrait of the man we knew. It has a degree of professionalism and eye for detail which would have produced a similar pride in Bill.

For those who didn't know him, the book will go a long way to explaining why he became such a tradition. I make no attempt to

vii

add to the anecdotes and, indeed, don't know that I could very much. Somehow our association, although very tempestuous, wasn't of that kind.

I'm proud to have the privilege to write this short introduction and to commend the book above all because it gives so successfully the portrait of the proud, passionate, dedicated, sincere and lovable man I had the joy of knowing.

PROLOGUE

BIG business in the Western world is tribal. It gathers itself into tight little enclaves, with clearly defined boundaries. It has customs and it has ritual—all of them slavishly obeyed. Though the mud huts have been replaced long, long ago by concrete and glass palaces, the primitive circumscription of territories remains. Thus the world of high finance has its Wall Street and its City; politics has its Westminster and its Washington; the law has its Old Bailey; advertising flourishes in Mayfair and on Madison Avenue.

This book is centred in one such tribal village—Fleet Street. But it is not about Fleet Street itself; rather it is about one of its better-known villagers—William Connor, 'Cassandra' of the *Daily Mirror*. In just over half a lifetime spent in the newspaper business, Bill Connor became an integral part of Fleet Street. The young brave turned—in the course of thirty-two years—into one of the tribal elders. It is, therefore, interesting to see what he thought of Fleet Street. He wrote this personal view two years before he died.

'Mother I have grave news for you. You must be brave.'
'What's happened?'
'It's about our Freddie.'
'Tell me what's happened—he's been hurt in an accident?'
'No, not exactly. But we must face this shock together.'
'Don't tell me he's in trouble with the police!'
'No—but it's sort of criminal!'
'Tell me! Tell me!'
'He's got a job.'
'What's the fuss? What's wrong with that?'
'Well, it's a very special kind of job—on . . . Fleet . . . Street.'
'Dear God . . .'
'Now steady Mother. We'll see this thing through . . .'
'But why did he do it? Why? Why? Why?'
'The shadow of tragedy comes into all our lives. But if we persevere we may yet see the light at the end of this dark corridor of time.'

'But we were good parents to Freddie. Look at the money we spent on his education. Why, he could have been a burglar. And then he goes to Fleet Street and brings shame and disgrace to our household and our name.'

'He could have been better than a burglar—he might even have become a train robber.'

'Or a blackmailer.'

'Perhaps an arsonist.'

'Or a drug addict.'

'Maybe even a pimp—or an abortionist.'

'How can I face the neighbours?'

'Steady, old girl. At least we have the consolation of telling Freddie that he will never darken our doors again. Fleet Street!'

I have been on Fleet Street for thirty years and I have never laughed so much. There is no other job like it, so absurd, so preposterous, so wildly improbable. The task which we impudently assume is to chronicle the whole pageant of life, to record the passing show and then, with unforgivable brazenness, to draw conclusions, to give a verdict and to point the moral. Damn and bless our bloody eyes.

I would never advise anyone to come to Fleet Street. Learning this trade is like learning high diving—minus the water.

But I wouldn't have missed it for all the treasures of Araby.

The man who, when he was asked what it was like to be in the First World War, said: 'Oh, the noise, AND THE PEOPLE!'

You can say the same thing about Fleet Street—'Oh, the noise, AND THE PEOPLE!'

You can get used to the noise but I've never got used to the people. The lovely nuts. The gorgeous crackpots. And all the wonderful, generous, self-derisive folk who spend their lives making dirty great black marks on miles and miles of white paper. Newspaper people are the greatest company in the world. They know, but they will never learn.

Fleet Street is a pavement where the manholes are missing. The aspirants who walk down it are warned by notices which say: 'CAUTION. MEN WORKING.' They stride on and in a trice are below ground. I know. I've done it.

Fleet Street is snakes-and-ladders. Fleet Street is the greasy pole with the old duck pond if you fall off. I know. I've done it.

The way to get on in Fleet Street is never let it be known that you want to. Hide Ambition's dark face. Never ascend the heights.

The newspaper business, especially in Fleet Street, is overshadowed by an angry, towering mountain, with the summit lost in the eternal hostile snows. Way down in the warm valleys below the foothills, life in the print business can be serene and relaxed. The place is stuffed with bee-loud glades where the idle, as well as the able, the incompetent as well as the efficient, can relax. The vegetation is thick and the great warm fronds provide shade for those who wish to lie in the noonday sun. Reporters, sub-editors, feature men and sports-writers can all have a relatively pleasant time and, if they wish, can make love to secretary birds under the kindly foliage.

A little further up the mountain, the foothills begin and the humming birds are no longer seen. The flowers are still bright, but there is a freshness in the air that old journalists suspect and young ones too often relish. Above the foothills you can see the sky between the trees.

Still further up, the foliage begins to diminish. There is a nip in the air and old hands shake their heads. The conifers grow shorter and stunted. The undergrowth thins out. Bushes take the place of trees, and there is little cover under which to hide. But the eager-beavers press on. Like young wild pigs they grunt and bolt around sniffing the freshening wind.

Far below, in the valley, there were flowers and berries and fruits to be found. Here there is little. Nor is the bark on the trees edible. But, still rooting and snorting, the ambitious porkers press on. It is the charge of the Gadarene swine in reverse—upwards instead of downwards—to disaster.

Above the bushes comes the scree. Above the scree come the boulders. Above the boulders, the snow-line. The ambitious journa-lists have thinned out now. Some are exhausted. Others are killed by their fellows. But here and there a burly brute, with a red gleam in a beady, angry eye that indicates the fevered image of the Editor's chair, still scrambles and scrabbles upwards.

I call them to come back. But it is too late, and as I stumble down the mountain to the softer climes below, I see the last of the Go-getters, the I-Believe-In-Me mob, struggling ever upwards. Little black dots slowly ascending the North Col.

Ultimately one of them makes it. O the power! O the glory! But they have still reckoned without the Abominable Snowman—the mysterious yeti, nine feet tall, covered in silky ginger fur with great gorilla-like feet leaving imprints in the dazzling snow. Sooner or later they meet him face to face and another familiar mountaineer has the millstone of Editorship round his neck and dies the death.

And the faithful Sherpas, who always knew that one glance from the Abominable Snowman meant disaster, were right.

Editors! I seen 'em come. And I seen 'em go. But way up on the mountain overshadowing Fleet Street the Abominable Snowman goes on for ever.

So, young stranger, my advice is don't come near us. Don't come on in 'for the water's warm'. It's not, it's hot. It's also freezing cold and it's rough too.

But it is the best, the finest, the most furious the most exciting bath of life that anyone could ever take.

But for Gawd's sake, mind the old plug 'ole.'

CHAPTER ONE

OPENING SCENE:
A NORTH LONDON SUBURB

ON the morning of 26 April 1909 the conductor of the Admiralty Glee Club—normally an extremely punctual man—was late for work. Like the classic Civil Servant, he was very much a creature of habit. And one of his habits was always to be on time. The gold half hunter he carried in his waistcoat pocket saw to that. But this time he was late—and very much so.

Not surprisingly his colleagues in the Pension Department were quick to notice the fact—and to speculate on it.

'I wonder if he's ill,' said one.

'I doubt it—he was very fit yesterday.'

'I expect his wife has presented him with twins', said a third, knowing that the conductor's wife was expecting a baby. The others laughed at this gentle piece of fun, and the conversation quietly lapsed. A short while later, the conductor arrived. In his soft Ulster voice he announced that his wife had indeed had twins—boys. At this his fellow workers, convinced that he was joking, broke into fresh laughter. It took him quite a time to persuade them that he was not pulling their legs.

When they realized that they were not the victims of a practical joke, they clustered round him, congratulating him on his good fortune.

'Both my hands go out to you, and my heart with them,' said a man called MacGregor, shaking him warmly by the hand.

Another colleague, Albert Davies, offered his best wishes and returned rather quickly to his work. Two days later he was to bring a bundle of baby clothes into the office and give them to the conductor, saying, 'Mrs Connor was probably not prepared for *two* children, so my wife and I have a small gift for you.'

The conductor of the Admiralty Glee Club was thirty-seven year old William Henry Connor. And one of the two boys that his wife had just had was to be christened William Neil by his parents and 'Cassandra' by the *Daily Mirror*. He was to do very much more than upset the time-keeping habits of a Civil Servant.

Bill (or Willie, as he was called by his parents) Connor's father was born in 1872 in the small town of Limavady near Lough Foyle in County Derry. He was the eighth of eleven children—five of whom died of T.B. in early childhood. Ireland was at that time going through a period of appalling poverty. Farmers with small-holdings were being evicted by the land owners. Every year thousands of Irishmen were emigrating to Canada and the United States. It was about this time that Parnell entered Parliament and became a prominent member of the Irish Home Rule party. Life was hard and Henry Connor's father, who was a schoolmaster, had a constant struggle to keep his family ade-quately fed and clothed. To add further to these difficulties, a Catholic school was opened up near his own. This was a severe blow, because the local priest insisted that all the Catholic children in the area should go to it, and since schoolmasters were paid on a per capita basis, his income fell drastically. He became a sad, embittered man and vowed that none of his children should suffer in the same way.

Henry Connor found this very awkward, since he had am-bitions to be a schoolmaster himself. Indeed, for a while when he was eighteen he helped his father by teaching in the school. But he finally gave way to parental pressure and went to Aberdeen to study for a business diploma.

He stayed in Aberdeen, living with family friends, for a couple of years, at the end of which he took, and passed, the entry examination for the Civil Service. Unknown to him, a young girl called Isabella Littlejohn was also studying at the same place. And she also was trying to get into the Civil Service. For a whole year their paths crossed; but it was not until a few years later in London that they were to meet and marry.

Isabella Littlejohn also came from a large family. Her father, a farmer at Tarves in Aberdeenshire, had married a cousin and they had had eight children, all girls. The people of the Buchan plain, north of Aberdeen, are a bluff and strong-willed lot. Arthur Littlejohn was no exception. He was certainly intensely disappointed that he had had no son to help him with the farm and to take it over from him; and so his daughters had a very strict and tough upbringing. The two eldest daughters were required to do the farm work of the sons that he had never had. But this had one good effect. It bred rebellion in the three youngest daughters. They had no wish to stay as unpaid help on the farm, and were determined to get away from farming at all costs. It was difficult, but they managed it. The three of them—Isabella, Rachel and Agnes—went to Aberdeen and it was there that Isabella studied commerce and eventually decided to enter the Civil Service.

By 1901 both William Henry Connor and Isabella Littlejohn were in London, he working as a clerk in the Pension Department of the Admiralty, and she as a telegraphist. They both lived in Islington and attended the Presbyterian Church in Colebrook Row—since pulled down—near Sadlers' Wells. And it was this that brought them together.

London has always had a magnetic attraction for people, and never more so than for people who are trying to get away from hard times and make a fresh start. And there were a great number of such people coming into London at the turn of the century. But having arrived in London they found it somewhat strange and a little frightening. Consequently they tended to stick together in little social groups, usually centred around something solid and familiar like a church. Islington at this time had quite a large community of expatriate Scots, and they got together as often as they could for outings and picnics and little parties. Isabella Littlejohn was part of one such group. She lived a quiet and socially respectable life. It was during this period that she first met Henry Connor—the man she was to marry. He was introduced to her by James Dickson, a mutual acquaintance, who was also a member of the congregation. There is no doubt that this little community was a warm and friendly one, for, in addition to their own meeting, three other couples, all close friends of theirs, met and married at about the same time.

Henry Connor and Isabella Littlejohn were married in the chapel at Barthol near her home at Tarves on 10 September 1902. James Dickson and the youngest sister, Agnes, were witnesses.

For a time after their marriage they lived in a small flat in

Holloway. Then in 1905 they moved to 52 Natal Road, N.11, where their first child, a daughter named Norah Elizabeth, was born.

Sixty years ago this part of North London was comparatively undeveloped. Many young families had moved out to enjoy the fields and trees while still being within easy reach of their work in London. The little triangle made up of Bowes Park, Palmers Green and Arnos Grove was full of the 'young marrieds' of the time. In the years since then, London has quietly crept up and overwhelmed this little suburb so that now it is virtually indistinguishable from any other part of North London. There are no frontiers any longer.

It was here, four years after their sister, that Bill Connor and his twin brother Mick were born. And it was here that they spent their early years.

In many ways a childhood spent in suburbia is a compromise. There *are* trees and grass, but they are usually in a park. A child can grow up knowing the names of every car and bus and lorry. But not the names of plants and flowers. Cows are things in picture books. Horses pull carts, not ploughs. Suburban life has its disadvantages—and its advantages.

One of those advantages for Bill Connor and his brother was, in fact, a park—Broomfield Park. It was here that they played a lot. There were conker trees (there still are), there were swings (there still are), there was even a discarded field gun (now thankfully, long gone). It had—and still has—the traditional pond, where fifty years ago a boy called Gilbert sailed his model yacht *Ulysses* to the extreme envy of all the other small boys. And it had its head park-keeper.

Mr Dunn was his name. He wore a thick black beard, a dark blue uniform and carried a stout walking stick. He played his part well. He looked fearsome, but had a heart of gold. Small boys—as they have always done—would beat down the conkers from the trees, but only when his back was turned; which was often enough to allow them to get a fair helping of the much-prized conkers, but not so often that the trees came to any great harm. The ominous looking walking stick was a symbol of authority that few dared to challenge. Mr Dunn 'walked softly and carried the big stick'—long before Harry S. Truman invented the phrase.

But childhood—unfortunately—is not simply a matter of playing in parks. It also includes school. The Elementary Education Act of 1870 set up what were known as Board Schools and, although the name was officially dropped in 1902, it clung on tenaciously for many years. And it was at the Board School in Bowes Road that Bill Connor and his brother first started their education. That was in 1914. For three years they stayed there, learning how to read and write and be baffled by arithmetic. In 1917 they moved to Franklyn House School in Palmerston Road. Franklyn House was one of the many double-fronted Victorian houses that abound in the area. It had originally been called Frankfort House, but, at the beginning of the 1914–18 war, because of public antipathy towards anything that sounded the least bit Teutonic, its name had been changed. It had three classrooms and about fifty pupils. The headmaster was a man named Heathfield, known universally to his charges as 'Pot'. 'Pot' was a pedant of the old order. He held prayers at the start and finish of every day. He had a particularly endearing habit, when teaching French, of insisting on pronouncing that language as though it were English. He showed it no mercy. Thus, if the French word for a swallow was 'une hirondelle', he would pronounce it 'oon highrondelly', regardless of the protests of his less forthright—though more Francophilic—colleagues. French was a language to be mastered—and master it he did! Indeed, so effective was his teaching that in later life many of his pupils had great difficulty in making themselves understood by Frenchmen. Including Bill Connor.

One of Bill Connor's friends at that time was a boy called Goulding who delighted both Connor boys with one of his inventions. It was a steam gun—a fiendish contraption made from a length of gas pipe, sealed at one end and with a bung at the other. Like most devices of its type it was simple in principle and very satisfying in operation. You simply put a little water in it, held it over a fire and waited. The water soon boiled, steam pressure built up and—bang—great roars of delight from small boys.

Bc

Like many twins, the Connor boys were full of mischief. Each egged on the other until something happened—something that usually aroused the disapproval or anger of a grown-up. In the early days of radio—when it was still called the wireless— Bill and his brother decided to build themselves a crystal set. But they found themselves without any wire for an aerial, and with no money to buy wire. So they solved their problem by taking the door-bell apart. In it they found yards and yards of red copper wire and they spent a whole afternoon stretching this back and forth from the roof of the house to a tree in the garden. The radio worked perfectly. The bell? Well . . . their father was not too happy about it.

As well as school and mischief there was something else that loomed large in their lives. Isabella Connor had been brought up, like so many Buchan Aberdonians, with a very healthy respect for 'the kirk'. Presbyterianism has always featured strongly in the religious life of Scotland and nowhere probably more strongly than in the north-east plain. And when she moved south she had brought her religion with her. Her husband also was a God-fearing man. Together, they and their children went twice—and sometimes three times—every Sunday to St James's Presbyterian Church. Fifty years ago it rattled to the thunder of some of the most militant and learned preachers. Now it rattles to the thunder of the lorries of the tea company who use it as a warehouse. The preaching was hard and vigorous. Any sermon there provided a full fifty minutes or more of good Scriptural meat. Words like 'darkness' and 'lightning' and 'cherubim' came whistling over the heads of the congregation like heavy artillery shells to land with devastating accuracy on the consciences of the two or three hundred unprotected souls. It was good stuff. Rich. Strong. God—at full throttle. And it had its amusing side. In an article Bill Connor wrote for the *Sunday Times* Magazine in 1964, he remembered an oft-repeated incident:

Visiting ministers to St James's who had never been there before had a peculiarly trying ordeal in store for them a few moments after they started their sermon. One of the most fearsome elders of our kirk . . . was deaf. He sat in the back pew rather like an emaciated

Moses. Ten seconds after the sermon from the stranger in the pulpit had started, he would rise to his feet and cup his ear with his right hand and then, slowly and majestically, walk down the aisle to the front pew where, with his hand still to his ear, he would listen to his ordained prey. It must have been a terrifying experience for the preacher and I have seen young Ministers falter and grow silent with their lips moving and no sound coming as they watched the merciless Elder bear down on them.

Every summer their parents would take young Willie and his brother and sister away for their holidays. They invariably went either to Portstewart, a small town near Limavady on the north coast of Ireland, or to Collieston, a tiny fishing village about fifteen miles north of Aberdeen. Both places had been childhood favourites of their parents, and both became favourites of their own. Part of the attraction was that going on holiday to either place meant seeing again favourite uncles and aunts and having small cousins to play with. The other thing that made these holidays so enjoyable was that, if they went to Scotland, there were five farms belonging to relatives that they could explore and enjoy. Lena Sexton, one of Bill Connor's cousins, remembers him at the time as being a very small, bright child with a prodigious memory. Arriving at the home of one of the uncles, he would spend about an hour going round the house like a dog sniffing new scents and would then come back and report exactly which pieces of furniture had been moved around and what was new to the home since his last visit a year or even two before. Invariably he was correct and this gift of a photographic memory was to be a great help to him in later life.

One of his particular favourites was his Uncle Charley, husband of Isabella Connor's second sister Jane. Uncle Charley was a thin, wiry Scots farmer with a prodigious thirst. One day when Bill was about five years old, he was taken down to the cellar of the farmhouse—a cellar which was always kept under lock and key. When they entered, he saw that it was packed from floor to ceiling with empty whisky bottles. With a great gleam of pride in his eye Uncle Charley said to him: 'You see a' those, Wullie? I drank 'em a' mysel'!' Uncle Charley's drinking came very near to being his downfall. One day he went to the local cattle market, and as was his custom, spent most of the day in a pub. He got spectacularly drunk and while in this state of insobriety, accidentally sold his farm to a friend. When next day the friend came round to collect the title deeds, Uncle Charley was unable to remember anything and denied it all as a hoax until the friend produced a piece of paper with his signature on it, agreeing to sell the farm. Uncle Charley was crestfallen—and he had to sell the farm. However, providence stepped in shortly after. There was a major recession in farming in the area and the man who had bought his farm lost virtually everything. Uncle Charley retired, bought another farmhouse, and made a lot of money dabbling on the Stock Exchange with the £15,000 he had from the sale of his farm. He was always delightfully eccentric in his habits. For instance, in a small wood on his farm he kept a wheel-less hansom cab. Every morning he spent a couple of hours sitting in the hansom cab reading the *Financial Times* and smoking his pipe. He made a lot of money—and drank a great deal of whisky. He was certainly the first of the eccentrics that Bill Connor so delighted in knowing, and collecting.

In September 1921, at the age of twelve, Bill Connor and his brother went to Glendale Grammar School in Wood Green. It was a big co-educational school with about 450 pupils. One of them was a boy called George Belcher—known to all his friends as Tubby because he was so much bigger than them all—who became a lifelong friend. Tubby Belcher remembers their first meeting in Mr Tate's science class: 'Bill Connor was a small, thin little boy who wasn't very good at mathematics so I helped him.' Bill Connor, in turn, later described Belcher as being 'a massive brain'. Belcher at that time was keen to start a school newspaper and tried to get all his friends to contribute. It was typed out, with innumerable carbon copies which got progressively more and more blurred. And it was short-lived. Belcher simply ran out of contributions from other people. He was particularly disappointed with Bill Connor's efforts. 'He used to give me some very bad jokes from an Irish joke book of his father's from time to time. I was amazed at how dreadful they were. I just could not inderstand how they made Bill roll about with laughter so much.' Not a very auspicious beginning for a man who was later to be a journalist of note.

Connor and Belcher soon became inseparable, although it was not simply a friendship during school hours. They forged strong links when they discovered that their parents read the *Daily News*, and soon they were having tea in each other's homes. The Connor boys were always glad to go to tea with Tubby because they were always given bananas. These they regarded as a special treat. It was not until many years afterwards that they discovered that this was as much a matter of expediency as of hospitality, Small boys are known for having huge appetites. The Connors were no exception. 'My mother had to give them bananas,' says Belcher, 'because they're so filling. Otherwise we'd have rapidly been eaten out of house and home.' Two or three evenings a week Bill Connor and Belcher would do their homework together. And usually 'the massive brain' would be required to help 'the thin little boy'.

During the holidays their mischief-making increased. The steam gun inspired them to greater explosions. They soon discovered that a certain explosive mixture, if wrapped tightly in a screw of paper and placed on the tram lines, went off with an impressive crack that startled the requisite number of passers-by. Keys were 'borrowed' and with the aid of a nail, some matches and a piece of string were turned into primitive hand grenades. Acetylene bombs were constructed. The neighbourhood was subjected to a seemingly never-ending series of explosions and violent noises throughout the holidays. It was particularly appropriate that Bill Connor should have been in the Royal Artillery during the war. After all, he had done most of the ground-work during this time.

The Connor twins were always getting up to something. Once they decided to clean their bicycle chains. The only solvent they had was petrol. And so they filled up one of their mother's best saucepans and put the oily chains in it. But it did not work quickly enough for their liking. So they put the saucepan—chains, petrol and all—on the gas stove. It was only their father's appearance on the scene that prevented a major disaster. He grabbed the boiling mixture from the stove and threw it out into the garden, where it demolished a neatly trimmed flower-bed.

When they were not getting up to mischief, the two boys were trying out all kinds of money-raising schemes. They used to help their father in his allotment by digging and weeding and carrying water for a farthing an hour. Then they hit upon a more lucrative idea with Tubby Belcher. Radio had just started and was very much the rage. 2LO and Savoy Hill were the magic words of the day. But wireless sets were both expensive and unreliable. So the boys started to make their own very simple sets with a cat's whisker and one valve. They were very good radio sets, if rather primitive, and they soon got orders from their school friends to make more. Then the parents of their friends started asking them for radios. Soon they had a small, flourishing and highly profitable business going.

Cars always fascinated the Connor boys. They used to vie with one another over the names and the respective merits of almost every car they saw. So when their father decided at long last to buy his first car they were delighted. Socially, of course, the motor car was an enormous asset at the time. People's success—or failure—was judged by the car they owned, and to a far greater degree than nowadays. Henry Connor decided to buy an A.C. As he was neither a very experienced nor a very good driver, he arranged for it to be collected by a friend of his, whom the two boys did not particularly like. However, this did not deter them from going with him; they wanted to see the new family pride and joy just as quickly as was possible. All went well up to a point. They collected the car and started back to Natal Road. Then, as they were coming down a steep hill to a major road-crossing, something suddenly went wrong. The friend who was driving tried to slow down at the road junction but forgot that the controls on the A.C. were different from those of his own car. So, instead of putting his foot on the brake, he trod very firmly on the accelerator. The A.C. shot forward into the main road and into the side of a tram. Luckily no one was hurt but the front of the car was badly crumpled. When they got home Henry Connor was furious. His brand new car—the one that he had not even driven—looked a very sorry sight as they pulled up outside his house. The friend was mortified. And the boys secretly chuckled at his plight.

Once they had a car in the family the two boys were irrepressible. They wrestled with one another for the privilege of sitting in the front beside their father. And they begged him to let them learn to drive. But he was adamant that they were too young and motorcars were very difficult and dangerous machines to control. He even resorted to keeping it under lock and key in the garage. This of course was a futile gesture. To start with, it was a little distance from the house. And then two teenaged boys with a mania for motorcars are more than a match for any padlock. They soon found a way into the locked garage. At first all they would do was to sit in the car and imagine themselves bowling along the open road. Then they became more adventurous. They would start up the car so that their dreams would have the correct sound effects and smells. Then they started to take the car out secretly, driving it around the neighbourhood in back streets lest they should be seen. Their mother, who was fully aware of what they were doing, kept their secret, though she was very fearful of what might happen if they accidentally damaged the car or themselves. Within a matter of months both boys were expert —if clandestine—drivers. And that was soon to be very useful.

One week-end Henry Connor took his family out for a drive. Mick was sitting in the front with him, Bill and his mother in the back. It had been a pleasant if bumpy journey—Henry Connor was an undistinguished driver—and they were nearing the top of a long climbing hill. Their father attempted a downward change into a lower gear, and failed. The car stopped and then began to roll backwards down the hill. Henry Connor began to panic. As one, the two boys leapt into action. Mick grabbed the steering wheel and put his feet on the pedals. Bill leant over from behind and worked the outside gear lever and handbrake. They stopped the car quickly, moved their father out of the driving seat and drove home. From that day, their father rarely drove the car himself. He was content to let his two sons take it in turns. And they were very happy to do so.

In 1926 Bill Connor left Glendale Grammar School. He had for some years prior to this been fascinated by the Navy, almost certainly because of his father's working association with the Admiralty. He therefore decided that he wanted to enlist.

Lacking the necessary academic qualifications, he went for a while to a crammer in Victoria to study for the Naval Entrance Exam. He said of it, at a later date, that 'it was the place where I learnt to drink and avoid hard work'. He sat the examination and passed, only to be turned down on medical grounds as he was not of the 'requisite optical standard'. Both he and his father were bitterly disappointed. He had not thought it possible that he would be refused and therefore had no other plans in mind for a career. But he had to do something and so he found himself a job at Derry & Toms in Kensington High Street. Ostensibly he was a trainee clerk. In fact, this meant that he was little more than a tea boy and broom-pusher in the accounts department. He found it completely soul-destroying and left after a couple of months.

By now he had vague ideas about accountancy as a career. Or rather, it would be truer to say that all the jobs he had during this doldrum period involved book-keeping and clerical work. He joined Asbestos Roofing Ltd and stayed with them for a while. He was still unhappy. His sister Norah had become a teacher. His brother was working as a musician on a P. & O. liner. His father was due to retire soon. And his mother was ill again. His youthful exuberance was dampened by the cold hard facts of life and an austere economy. Then in 1929 he answered an advertisement in a newspaper for a clerk in the accounts department of an advertising agency called Arks Publicity. Though he could not know it at the time, it was going to be the start of his career as a writer.

It was also about this time that a very real tragedy struck the Connor family. Shortly after the birth of Bill Connor's elder sister Norah, his mother had a nervous breakdown. It was a simple mental reaction brought on, no doubt, by post-child-birth depression. It was one that would certainly be easily dealt with today. But at that time mental illness was very little understood and not easily treated. She was ill for a time and then seemed to have recovered.

One day in 1926 when he was seventeen, Bill Connor came home from work and smelt gas on entering the house. He rushed into the kitchen and found his mother lying on the floor unconscious, with the oven gas taps on. He dragged her out and an ambulance was called. Luckily he had found her in time.

His mother's attempted suicide made a very deep impression on Bill Connor and on the rest of the family. All his life he had a horror of suicide, having seen one, mercifully unsuccessful, attempt in his own home.

This second illness of his mother's was far more serious than the first. For the next ten years, until about 1937, she received treatment for it, both in and out of hospitals. She was finally discharged as cured; but it was not to be the final chapter in her story.

CHAPTER TWO
A YOUNG MAN GETS A JOB

ARKS Publicity was a small company with offices in Lincoln's Inn Fields. It was a great breeding place for talent. Sir Alec Guinness worked there for a while, Philip Zec the cartoonist was an art director there, and it was the place where Bill Connor first started writing. The managing director— C. O. Stanley—was also a man of great ability and later became chairman of Pye of Cambridge. And it was he, in a roundabout fashion, who was responsible for causing Bill Connor to become a writer.

In a company as small as Arks was at that time, everyone knows exactly what everyone else does. And sometimes, of necessity, everyone finds himself doing a bit of someone else's job as well as his own. This was the case with Connor. For, in addition to looking after ledgers and ordering advertisement blocks, he often wrote small bits of copy for advertisements himself. Most were done for his own amusement. However, he was also neglecting his work so that one day he was summoned by C. O. Stanley and asked if he could write advertising copy.

'I don't know,' was the honest reply.

'Well, you've got a month to find out. If by the end of it you're no good, then you're out,' said Stanley.

Needless to say Bill Connor kept his job.

Philip Zec had joined Arks Publicity straight from the St Martin's School of Arts in Charing Cross Road. He was already working as a layout artist when Bill Connor turned writer and remembers his first sight of him. 'A very thin little man with round glasses and hair parted in the middle came into my room with a piece of copy that he had written. He gave it to me and asked me what I thought of it. I was fully prepared to take this upstart clerk down a peg or two. But then I read it—and it was very good.' It was an advertisement for a lift company and was the first of many that Zec and Connor did together. It was also the start of a working partnership that was to be continued later at the *Daily Mirror* and the beginning of a deep and close friendship that was to last right up to Connor's death.

The two of them rapidly built up a great respect for each other's work. On one occasion Connor came into Zec's room and was idly flipping through some layouts when he came across some that stopped him. They were a campaign for 'Mullard, the master valve', and Zec had been experimenting with a technique known as air-brushing in which ink is sprayed on to the paper with a miniature spray gun. It was a technique that Bill Connor had not come across before and he was much impressed by it. At first he did not believe that Zec had done them. 'They're too good,' he said. After some time, and with great difficulty, Zec managed to convince him that he had done them.

'In that case I shall have to re-write my copy,' said Connor, and went off to do so. He had to make sure that the copy was fully as good as the layouts. Out of this episode came the 'I am a radio wave' campaign which was greeted with much acclaim at the time.

Bill Connor always had a great fondness for Arks Publicity. He liked it as a place to work. And he liked the people there, especially when Tubby Belcher came to join them as a writer in 1932. He had one particularly favourite anecdote which he used to tell about Arks. C. O. Stanley from time to time would have a drive on punctuality. The normal procedure was that everyone had to sign on in a book. A line would be drawn across the page at 9 o'clock and anyone who arrived after that could be spotted immediately. However, the staff soon found a way round this by leaving plenty of space between the names above the lines so that anyone arriving late would have room to put his name in. But then Stanley foiled this little subterfuge by standing by the door as they came in. Moreover, he took to informing anyone who arrived late that his services would no longer be required. This would have been disastrous but for the fact that by mid-afternoon he invariably softened and sent round a memorandum informing all the members of the staff he had fired in the morning that they were 'hereby reinstated'. In this way Connor was himself fired and re-hired at least half a dozen times and always claimed that no one was really a full member of Arks Publicity until he had been through the same procedure.

About the time that Bill Connor joined Arks Publicity his family moved from their house in Natal Road to Carshalton Beeches, near Sutton in Surrey. Here they bought a house in Banstead Road. His mother's health was still bad; she was suffering from the same depression that had caused her to attempt suicide some years before. Time after time she went into hospital in Northampton for treatment. It was usually successful but only for short periods. His father thought that the move further away from London would do her some good and he appeared at first to be right. Bill and his brother lived at home and travelled up to town by train every day. Their sister was by now teaching in a local school.

One day, about six months after the Connor family had moved into Banstead Road, they saw some people looking at the vacant house next door. Henry Connor—or Pa as he was universally known—went out to talk to them and asked them if they would like the keys to the house, which had been left with him by the local estate agent. They said yes, looked round the house, were delighted with it and soon bought it and moved in. It was not until much later that they found out that Pa Connor had only offered the keys to people who he thought would make good next-door neighbours. The couple who moved in were George and Margaret Reed and they had a very young son called Peter. The Reeds and the Connors soon became firm friends. Until then the Reeds had lived all their lives in London and found living in the country—as it still was at that time—vastly different. Pa Connor, who was a very keen gardener, helped. He told them what to plant in their garden and when to plant it. One day they very proudly showed him some 'apple trees' which they had bought from a passing salesman. He took one look at them and said, 'They're not apple trees, they're beech', and the next day presented them with three proper apple trees as a gift.

Pa Connor was an impulsive giver of gifts, and sometimes they turned out to be not quite as expected. He had a big Airedale terrier called Derry, known and respected by all the tradesmen in the area because of his appetitite for trouser legs. During one holiday Peter Reed looked after Derry for the Connors. When they returned, Pa was so delighted at the expert way that Peter had looked after his dog that he asked George and Margaret Reed if he might give Peter a puppy of his own. They were delighted and readily agreed to his request. Two days later they were called to the window by a very excited Peter. They looked out to see a harassed Pa Connor being towed down their garden path by a fully-grown Airedale. Some puppy!

Though they were by now in their early twenties the two Connor twins had not lost much of their exuberance. Pa went round complaining about their staying out late and disapproving of their going into pubs and of their drinking. He tried to be a very strict father. He had strong ideas about the bringing up of children. But he had one characteristic that weakened his every argument—a very nicely developed sense of humour. Though he tried to be stern, it would not—or could not —last for long because he would burst out laughing at his own seriousness. All the same he was much put upon by his two sons. He demanded that they should be home by a certain time if they went out in the evening. So to circumvent his anger if they came home late, they kept a rope under one of the beds. It was then very simple for the one who came home latest to toss a stone against the window to wake up the other, who would in turn throw out the rope so that the late-comer could get in without having to face father. Pa, of course, knew all about this but could never catch them in the act. And whenever he asked George or Margaret Reed if they had seen or heard anything they would deny it. 'We covered up for the two of them time and time again,' they recalled.

Very often, when their mother was in hospital, Pa would spend week-ends visiting her. When this happened, Bill and Mick took advantage of it. 'We used to hear the piano being played the whole week-end,' said the Reeds. Tubby Belcher was a frequent visitor to Banstead Road for these week-ends, partly because he was an expert piano player, and also because he was a workmate of Bill Connor's at Arks. He recalled one particular week-end that he and Bill spent at Carshalton Beeches. It was in the summer and the Friday was a very hot day indeed, particularly inside their office. Everyone was thirsty but no one had any money to buy a drink. Then Bill Connor found a tin of Eno's Fruit Salts in the office and decided that since it was fizzy it would help quench their thirsts. So he helped himself to a glass, despite Tubby's warnings about its laxative properties. And then another. And another. In all he must have drank about a half tin of the stuff. As they left the office, the Eno's started taking effect. They had just got on a bus to London Bridge when suddenly Bill Connor leapt off and rushed to the nearest public lavatory. 'We didn't get home until about 9 o'clock that evening because we had to stop off at every station along the way,' said Belcher.

This was only the start of the week-end. They arrived home to find the kitchen virtually bare of food. And they had practically no money between them because they had spent it on stocking up with beer. They could not get credit with any of the local shops because Pa had expressly forbidden it and warned the local shopkeepers against them. And they were very hungry.

> After about a half-hour spent searching round the house we found two eggs and some potatoes. We peeled the potatoes and Bill said he'd make some scrambled egg. He was fooling around with one of them and I told him to be careful or else he was likely to break it. Suddenly he dropped it and it smashed on the floor. I was annoyed. He just laughed and started throwing the remaining egg up in the air and catching it, saying he would not drop this one. But of course he did, so all we had left was a plate of potatoes and lots of beer.

Despite this, it was an enjoyable week-end.

1932 was a year of great upheaval in the Connor household. Pa Connor retired from the Admiralty at the age of 60. His wife had been ill and was still away in Northampton. Brother Mick had taken up a career as a music hall artist, following his job with P. & O. Norah was now living in Cheam and teaching in Surbiton. Because the family were so scattered around the country, Pa decided to sell the house in Banstead Road. This he did in the early part of 1932. For a few months he lived in Norah's flat in Cheam and then found and rented a cottage in the small village of Wheeler End, about six miles from High Wycombe in Buckinghamshire. In the same year Bill Connor left Arks and found himself a flat in London.

He had again answered a newspaper advertisement—this time

placed anonymously by the J. Walter Thompson advertising agency. At his interview he told his prospective employers that he had known who they were from the advertisement because of the style of typeface they had used. Whether or not this impressed them sufficiently to give him the job is a matter for conjecture. He merely seemed proud to have been able to volunteer the information. And he was delighted to get the job. C. O. Stanley was not too happy to lose him and said so. But the attraction of £450 a year salary and the chance of working in a company which even then was highly respected in the advertising industry was more than Connor could resist. He joined them in mid-1932.

J. Walter Thompson—or JWT as it is known to all and sundry in the advertising industry—is one of the oldest and biggest of the advertising agencies in Britain. It is, in fact, of American parentage, being an offshoot of a world-wide organization which was originally started by a retired American Naval Commander just before the turn of the century. For some reason best known to itself, it has always managed to stand a little aloof from other advertising agencies. When they have been going through lean times in business, JWT has prospered. When others have prospered, JWT has not done so well. And it has always been a refuge for poets and playwrights and odd characters, and has had more than its fair share of them as a result. Sometimes it appears ultra-professional; at other times it appears as though it is staffed by eccentric madmen. It is a fascinating place with fascinating people.

Within a matter of days of joining JWT, Bill Connor had met one of the most fascinating men JWT has ever produced—Basil D. Nicholson; a man who could outrage and charm in the same moment of time; a man who lived his life at a fierce rate—and got every last drop out of it; and a man who featured high on Connor's list of eccentric friends. Nicholson had come into advertising almost by accident. He had been to Oxford and had drained it of all that it had to offer him. In looking around for new fields, he had discovered advertising. It appealed to him both for its apparent lunacies and its in-built excitement. It was a challenge —and he met it. He also wrote a pot-boiler called *Business is Business* which Hugh Cudlipp describes in *Publish and be Damned* as 'a book . . . full of wit, confusion and downright brilliant nonsense', a description that fits the book well, and the man who wrote it even better.

Bill Connor, in the only published obituary to appear after Nicholson's death in 1953, said of him:

> Ninety per cent of the people who met him did not understand him, were afraid of him or hated him with a violence that he was first to applaud for its virulence. But the other ten per cent?
> I was one of them. We were very very fond of him. We relished the wounding wit. We loved his handling of the impossible. We delighted in the extravagance of this rasping, sarcastic bomb of endless ideas, each of which demanded one whole new world to conquer.

Without doubt Nicholson had a great influence on Connor. He opened the door of his experience and life at Oxford to Connor who had never had the opportunity to go to a university. From him, no doubt, Connor learnt some of the finer points of invective, an art in which he, the pupil, later outshone his teacher. Above all Nicholson expanded Connor's mental horizons.

Nicholson was an extraordinarily far-sighted man. Much of the work that he initiated was only recognized long after he had moved on to other things. For instance, he was the inventor of the famous Horlicks 'Night Starvation' phrase, coupled with the strip cartoon treatment of it, a phrase that only became famous after he had left advertising and which lasted a great deal longer than he did. He had an outrageous sense of humour and was always willing to poke fun at the things he did. He was peculiarly fond of ridiculing the advertising industry. One story in particular shows this. At the time that he and Connor were working at JWT, they were advertising a brand of tinned salmon. The most popular brand at the time was John West's which was—and still is—a rich deep pink in colour. Nicholson hit upon the idea of selling their client's competitive salmon as 'the only salmon that doesn't turn red in the tin'. At the time it was regarded as a preposterous idea and utterly unthinkable. It is interesting to note that a great deal of present-day advertising uses exactly this approach—one of gently taking a wry poke at the product being advertised.

Nicholson became the silently-acknowledged ring-leader of a small group of writers and artists at JWT. Lunchtimes would be spent inventing new ways of making money over large quantities of beer at Henekey's in the Strand. Or in making and accepting absurd bets on trivial things. One such bet that Nicholson made was when he had watched Bill Connor eat a three-course luncheon. Nicholson said that he could not do that again, and bet the cost of a second lunch on it. Connor accepted the challenge and solemnly waded through another three courses—brown windsor, meat and two veg, and a sweet.

Connor and Nicholson were always trying to find new ways to make money. They invented a whole host of gadgets, one of which—a set of three skewers with hooks on the end called Carver Grips which held a joint fixed on the plate—was eventually manufactured and sold quite well over two or three years. They soon came to the conclusion that if they were to go into business properly they would need to form a limited company. So in 1934 they formed Campbell Craig and Company, the name being chosen because they felt it sounded reliable and respectable. The joke was further compounded by another of their schemes a couple of years later. They decided to make and sell a fake aphrodisiac, a mixture of cold tea and passion fruit juice, under the name of Craig's Theol. They bottled gallons of the stuff and kept it in Connor's flat. They decided to advertise it. Connor wrote this advertisement:

YOU WANT TO BE LOVED!

Get the secret arousing charm

It's not beauty that wins in the race for men—it's the FLATTERING WAYS, the CHARM, and the DESIRABILITY that comes from QUICKENED SENSES.

You *too* can have a husband.

You *too* can be flattered, sought after, taken out. The subtle potency of Craig's Theol can turn an unattractive 'Wallflower' almost immediately into a woman of FATAL ALLURE.

The secret? The special Eastern Ingredients in Craig's Theol make you feel ready for love—make you react quicker in those ways that make women DESIRED BY MEN. Are you lonely? Do you love one

Cc

who shows no response? Is your lover—your husband slipping away?
Once your senses are quickened you will be loved again. Craig's
Theol is absolutely harmless. Craig's Theol is tasteless in tea. Send
P.O. 2/6d. (money back if not satisfied) for a full sized bottle of
Craig's Theol (Post Free) to. . . .

They imagined themselves rapidly becoming rich through a
multiplicity of half-crowns sent in by unhappy spinsters, eager to
be loved. They roared with laughter at their cleverness and their
daring. Unfortunately for them (though fortunately, no doubt,
for the spinsters) no newspaper or magazine would print their
advertisement for them. 'We do not think it necessary to explain
why the advertisement sent would not be acceptable to the
proprietors of this excellent woman's weekly,' wrote *The Red
Letter*. Even *Titbits* turned them down.

Bill Connor, doubtless egged on by the maniac jibes of Nicholson, became known as a practical joker at J. Walter Thompson.
Bob Scanlan, who then as now worked at JWT, tells of the time
when the then managing director, a mysterious and somewhat
awesome American named Ray Smith, was having—like C. O.
Stanley—a blitz on time-keeping. This annoyed Connor and
Nicholson immensely, so much so that Connor came in one
morning absolutely on the dot of 9.30, picked up the phone and
dialled Ray Smith's internal number. Smith picked it up and heard
a voice say, 'Ray?' 'Yes?' he replied, slightly puzzled. 'Oh, it's
all right. I just wanted to know if you were in,' said Connor, and
put down the phone. Smith never knew who the mystery voice
was.

On another occasion Connor had a telephone joke played on
him. An art director named William Larkins, the man who
designed the original and famous Black Magic chocolate box,
rang him up from his office upstairs and asked him about a piece
of copy that Connor had written. 'I don't think it's very good,'
said Larkins. Connor was very painstaking with his writing and
to be told that any piece was inferior was like a red rag to a bull.
He immediately launched into a huge and vulgar tirade against
Larkins, who quietly put the phone down on his desk, came down
to Connor's room and stood silently beside him. He waited a

few moments while Connor continued to rant, then coughed quietly to attract his attention. Connor looked up, his face a picture of confused, perplexed wrath.

Towards the end of 1933 Basil Nicholson became a little restless. Advertising was losing its grip on him. The excitement was a little less intense, the attraction not so strong. He became a little impatient and started to look around for new things to interest him and—more importantly—to earn the fortune that had up till then escaped him. He became obsessed by the strip cartoon. It was a technique that he had applied with great success to Horlicks. He made a study of strips. The New York *Daily News* was at that time the only newspaper in the world of any note that used strip cartoons. It became almost a bible for him. Very soon he realized that the time was ripe for cartoons of this type to be introduced to the British public, and that it was possible that the man who made the introduction could make money out of it. His enthusiasm was highly infectious; Bill Connor joined him in his project. Together they hatched a scheme. They would produce a strip cartoon of their very own. And they would sell it to a newspaper. The problem was what kind of strip should they produce—and who would buy it.

The first problem they solved quickly—by producing two. There was an American named Ripley who was famous for his strip, a collection of unusual and interesting facts presented in drawings under the heading 'Believe it or not?'. No one had anything to approach it in Britain—so that was one to be plagiarized. After a decent interval spent in camouflaging the Ripley idea and adding a few variations of their own, Connor and Nicholson produced the first 'Nikkon' strip. The name, rather obviously, was a combination of their two surnames and the strip itself a collection of general knowledge facts not quite so obscure as the Ripley strip. Philip Zec, who was running his own studio at the time, was called in to provide the drawings.

The second strip was called 'Queer People: Famous Oddities Of All Time', and featured a short pictorial history of such fascinating characters as Jemmy Hirst, the Doncaster leather-merchant of the 1840s, who went hunting mounted on a bull.

The 'Nikkon' strip was sold to the *News Chronicle*; the 'Famous

Oddities' appeared in the *Sunday Express*. Both lasted for well over six months.

These strip cartoons were—though they were not to know it —key factors in a chain of events that was to lead to them both joining the *Daily Mirror*. As it happened the *Daily Mirror* was at the time a client of J. Walter Thompson, and Nicholson knew the man who was then the Publicity Director of the paper. His name was Cecil Harmsworth King. Nicholson approached King with the idea that what the *Daily Mirror* needed badly at that time was a strip cartoon and that he, Nicholson, had some ideas, and was Mr King interested? Mr King was.

Very shortly afterwards Nicholson and Connor became contributors to the *Daily Mirror*. Nicholson fed idea after idea, each more extravagant and expansive than the last, into the *Mirror*. Connor wrote articles from time to time, all of which he submitted to the *Mirror*, some of which were used, though he never saw his name (nor wanted it, since JWT would have been very angry) at the top of the piece. They were very happy to have found such a useful outlet for their freelance activities and it is doubtful whether they really cared about carrying their newspaper interests much further. They may have had the occasional idea of becoming newspapermen but the hard financial facts of life about the *Mirror* probably dissuaded them. The *Mirror*, started in 1903 by Lord Northcliffe, an uncle of Cecil King, as a daily newspaper for 'gentlewomen', was in a sad and sorry state. It had been losing circulation at a remorseless rate. In 1934 it had dropped as low as 730,000 readers, very nearly a million readers less than the *Daily Express* at that time. The management were very worried. All their remedies had met with failure. The line on the graph marked 'Circulation' just would not turn and move up. It became a case for surgery, not therapy. Cecil King suggested that the time had come for a new Publicity Manager. In suggesting this, he had Basil Nicholson in mind. So in 1935 Nicholson was offered the job. He accepted it. It offered a new challenge and fresh fields for him to conquer. But the *Mirror* were not to know quite what they had bought in hiring Nicholson. He was a great anti-establishment man. Almost his first act on joining was to infuriate the first of many *Daily Mirror* directors, a man named

Wallace Roome, by ringing him up and demanding a desk and a red telephone. By the time he left Nicholson was to have incensed just about the whole Board and about ninety per cent of the staff of the paper.

Nicholson took with him, within months of joining the *Daily Mirror*, quite a few of the people he had been working with at J. Walter Thompson. And one of them was his avid disciple, Bill Connor. It was never quite clear at first exactly what Connor was supposed to do, beyond some kind of writing stint. He had certainly not been hired with the specific intention of writing the Cassandra column. That decision was taken a few days after he arrived.

In order fully to appreciate the effect of the influx of men like Nicholson in 1935, it may be useful at this juncture to consider the position of the *Mirror* at that time. It was suffering from poor circulation. Apart from Harry Guy Bartholomew, previously the editor and by then a director, Cecil Thomas, who was the editor at the time, and a young and, as yet, untried, Cecil King, the *Daily Mirror* management were fairly unremarkable. Most of the rest of the Board were men who had been there quite some time. A few of them had been noteworthy in their day but were now resting on their laurels. It was, perhaps most of all, suffering from a lack of identity. It had failed as a ladies' newspaper. In the 1920s, when everyone else was involved in the new and shocking flapper age, it stayed aloof and proclaimed, in a still, small voice, the qualities of gentility. It had undertaken hare-brained schemes like football-pool competitions and free life insurance in a succession of desperate attempts to attract readers. It was like a ship dismasted, helpless and carried hither and thither by managerial decisions which were mutually contradictory. To carry the metaphor further, Bartholomew was like the first officer on a ship whose captain lay below, suffering, even dying. He knew what he should do, but the crew were not yet listening to him. The old team had failed; it was time to bring in the new.

What the new team did bring to the *Daily Mirror* was ideas. Brilliant ones. Stupid ones. Simple ones. And complicated ones. Good, bad and indifferent ones. But above all, plenty of them. In the main, most of the people who joined in 1935 had little if any experience in newspapers. And this is almost certainly why they succeeded. They were not hidebound. If someone said, with the wisdom of many years spent in the dying *Mirror*, 'You can't do *that*!', they would say, 'Why not?'. They were also young—and brash. Whilst they could not immediately imagine themselves as being successful in a business of which they knew little, they were certainly confident that they would never be failures. They had a lot to learn about newspapers, but they felt that newspapers had a lot to learn from them. Almost everything they did, right from the start, was certain to end in the slaughter of sacred cows and the crushing of someone's corns. It was an attitude to life and business that they had learnt from working in advertising. That business has always thrived on flamboyance and a questioning attitude. They had simply taken it with them to their new jobs.

They also had one other factor in their favour—luck. The men who were responsible for hiring them were brave enough to take a gamble and to give them the opportunities that they so ably grasped. Without this piece of good fortune there is little doubt that the *Daily Mirror* would have ceased publication and that many people's reputations would never have been made. Freedom of expression was what they had been looking for; freedom of expression was what they were given.

CHAPTER THREE

FIRST GLANCE IN THE MIRROR

THE week of August Bank Holiday 1935 was, apart from some sabre-rattling by the Italians in Ethiopia, a fairly quiet one. Mr Walter Elliott, the Minister of Agriculture, announced that the Government's sugar policy stayed much as before and that the subsidy on sugar beet was to continue indefinitely. Dr Frick, the German Minister of the Interior, announced that labour service for girls was now compulsory in Germany. In Uruguay gold was revalued, while in Holland the bank rate was reduced. Prosperity seemed to be creeping back to some parts of the world after the dark days of the Depression. In South Africa they developed a vaccine for horse sickness. The highest road in Europe, the Grossglockner, was opened. The Russians were having a little local difficulty on their border with Mongolia. Liberals from all over the world were in London for an international conference. The County Bank and the District Bank announced a merger. Mr T. O. M. Sopwith's 'Endeavour' won the King's Cup at Cowes Regatta. Twelve police constables were enrolled as Britain's first flying police at Reigate flying club. And Bill Connor, Hugh Cudlipp and Peter Wilson joined the *Daily Mirror*.

All three, in fact, joined on the same day, August Bank Holiday Monday. Connor had followed Basil Nicholson from J. Walter Thompson. Peter Wilson had followed in his father's footsteps and joined the *Mirror* as a sports writer, a job which earned him the slightly wincing title of 'The Man They Can't Gag'—a title typical in its arrogance of the brash young *Daily Mirror*. Hugh Cudlipp had followed the Sits Vac Columns of the *Daily Telegraph* and had been given the job of Assistant Features Editor advertised there by Basil Nicholson. When Nicholson had interviewed Cudlipp he had said that he didn't think he would last much longer at the *Mirror* and asked Cudlipp if he could start that very day, 'Otherwise I might be fired before you get here.' Cudlipp got there just as soon as he was able.

One of the first things that happened to Bill Connor on his arrival was that he met Harry Guy Bartholomew—known to all as 'Bart', and feared by most. Until that moment 'Bart' had merely been a name to Connor, 'one of the Board'. His first meeting with him was to change that rapidly. It was short—and it was sharp, like the man himself. Connor told the tale himself in an obituary he wrote after Bartholomew's death in 1962.

> He gave me my first newspaper job and the interview was characteristic. Said 'Bart': 'Can you write a column?' Like the man who was suddenly asked if he could play the violin, I replied; 'I don't know. I've never tried.' He said 'Start now!'—and sure enough I've been sawing the catgut ever since.

Bartholomew had joined the *Daily Mirror* in 1904, the year after it had been founded and when it had a daily circulation of around 25,000 copies—When he left, in 1951, it had grown to more than four and a quarter million. He had started as assistant art editor to the great Hannen Swaffer. When he left, he was Chairman of the *Daily Mirror*. Bart looked like a white-haired bulldog—and had a temperament to match. He was tenacious and a man of instinct. Like the bulldog he would sniff out the friend or the enemy. He recognized the smell of talent—and found it in the most unlikely people. Bart was no smooth, well-groomed operator. He had learned the newspaper business by getting ink on his hands many times. He could also be a very warm man. The iron glove contained a velvet hand, which was proffered to those he liked or respected—not always the same things to Bart. Again, from the obituary which Connor wrote:

> He was hard as nails, and as soft as butter. He was sentimental and gritty, tender—yes tender—and tough as the lash of the sjambok.
> He was horseradish sauce and honey, barbed wire and blue ribbon. . . . In his way Bart was easily the most formidable newspaperman I ever met. He was a revolutionary all right and he dearly loved a fight. With many others who knew him well—and he needed some knowing—I mourn a volcano. And a big one at that.

Virginia Vernon, who was formerly the Paris Correspondent of the *Daily Mirror*, tells of a time early in 1941 when she lived in a flat at St James's Court. She shared a bathroom with an elderly couple who had the room next to hers. Her name was Bertha; his was Guy. They actually lived in the luxurious flat on the top floor but had taken the room for their own greater security and also to provide a safer repository for an enormous collection of china shepherds and shepherdesses, china lambs, china cats and china dogs by the dozen, some priceless, some worthless.

Guy was always out during air-raids, dressed in full fireman's outfit, and after the all-clear had gone he would return triumphant. His attitude seemed to indicate that he felt he had put out all the fires himself and had sent the German bombers packing. He would cry out, 'Tea . . . let's have some Scotch!' He appeared to have an unlimited supply of rationed whisky which he would pour out in great triple helpings for Virginia Vernon and himself; his wife never drank. He would then goad Virginia Vernon into talking abour France—a country that she loves dearly and which he loathed. He dismissed France and the French summarily. 'The French are bastards!' he shouted. One particular display of verbal pyrotechnics was about Léon Blum, leader of the Front Populaire who had exposed and imprisoned a fascist named Eugène de l'Oncle. The occupying German forces had then released de l'Oncle and imprisoned Blum. Virginia Vernon was almost in tears: 'He's a patriot,' she cried. Guy leaned forward, cheeks flushed. 'I don't believe a goddam word you say,' he said. 'Will you write it for my paper?'

'What paper?'

'The *Daily Mirror*. I am a Director. My name is Bartholomew. Call me Bart.'

Another story about the Bart brand of nitro-glycerine eloquence. At the beginning of the war the *Daily Mirror*, through its 'Live Letters' page, had a drive to get musical instruments for the troops. It was so successful that Bill Connor and Philip Zec found themselves sharing their room with a huge assortment of instruments, including a harmonium, a guitar and a set of drums. Zec had in fact only joined the *Daily Mirror* a matter of weeks before and was very new to the place and its personalities. After one particular pub lunch he and Connor decided to amuse themselves by playing 'Sweet and Low', with Connor on the harmonium and Zec on the guitar. Within minutes of their duet starting a man named Arthur Fuller, Financial Director of the paper at that time, burst through the door demanding to know what all the noise was about and didn't they know that there was a war on and that they were supposed to be running a paper, not a band?

'We're having a jam-session,' explained Zec to the unknown who had intruded. 'I'm playing the guitar, Bill's playing the harmonium and do you by any chance happen to play the drums?'

Fuller retired, slamming the door. Zec's face fell when Connor informed him that they had just insulted a director of the company.

Two minutes later, the door burst open—again in mid-chorus —and in stormed a small, white-haired hurricane.

'What the hell is all this bloody row?' he demanded.

Zec, summoning all his patience, as though he were talking to a particularly obtuse child, explained carefully to this second stranger that he was playing the guitar, Connor was playing the harmonium, that the tune was 'Sweet and Low' and did he by any chance have any skill on the drums?

'Of course I can bloody well play the drums!' roared Bart and sat down to play with them.

'He was terrible,' recalls Zec, 'but we had a great afternoon.'

Both Connor and Zec liked Bart. When Virginia Vernon finally joined the staff of the *Daily Mirror* in 1946, Bart said to her, 'There are two madmen you must meet. One is a Russian Jew named Philip Zec, the other is an Irish heathen named William Connor. Zec is the best cartoonist in the British press, Bill Connor is the finest columnist in the world. He signs *Cassandra*. He is a genius. I love the bastard . . . I think he loves me. Get to know him. Get to know them both. They are as different as chalk and cheese. They are friends. Make them like you . . . you *can* be likeable, you know. And so can they.'

Every brilliant man needs a foil; something or someone who provides the necessary contrast which makes any assessment of that man possible. And if Harry Guy Bartholomew can be said to have had a foil it was Cecil Harmsworth King. Bart was short. King is tall, amazingly so. Bart was voluble. King gives one the impression at first of having received a crash course in small-talk at a Trappist monastery. Bart was volatile. King is imperturbable. Bart was a rough diamond. King has the polish of the Wykehamist. Bart trusted his instinct about people and situations. King is the careful analyst. Bart ran on blood pressure. King runs on brain power.

Cecil King was born in 1901. His father was Sir Lucas King who, before he became Professor of Oriental Languages at Trinity College, Dublin, had been a Civil Servant in India. His uncle was Lord Northcliffe who had started the *Daily Mail* and was later the owner of *The Times*. Cecil King went to school at Winchester. From Winchester he went to Christ Church, Oxford. On coming down from Oxford, King made the first move into what was to become a momentous career in the newspaper business. He joined the *Glasgow Record*. He then spent three years working in the advertising department of the *Daily Mail*. In 1926 he moved to the *Daily Mirror*. Three years later he was appointed to the Board. By 1935 he was the director in charge of advertising.

On the face of it it seems impossible that two men as dissimilar as King and Bartholomew should ever have come together in normal circumstances. But the circumstances were far from normal. In the middle 1930s they were the only two members of the Board who were not simply interested in preserving the fading respectability of the *Mirror*. They were more interested in preserving the *Mirror* itself. Unlike John Cowley, the Chairman, they cared not a fig about what their friends at their clubs might think. Rather, they cared about what the Official Receiver might think.

Stories of Cecil King are harder to find than stories about Bartholomew. But this in itself may provide an important clue to the man himself. He is not at all forthcoming. Indeed, it is very easy to have a marvellously one-sided conversation with him. But behind the taciturn exterior the mental scales are at work—weighing, balancing, assessing. Indeed, as Hugh Cudlipp says in *Publish and Be Damned*, many an executive or newspaperman has been invited to accompany King on business trips abroad and has had his character, opinions and knowledge carefully probed and examined, unbeknown to him. King's philosophy must surely be to watch and observe. You learn a lot more about a man by looking at him than by just listening to him. This approach may of course be due to the fact that King is basically a shy man. But it may also have something to do with the impish sense of humour that close associates have found in him. It is not for nothing that the Harmsworth family originally came from the land of the leprechaun.

It is a little surprising to learn that during his first few years at the *Daily Mirror* Bill Connor was not in fact on the proper salaried staff; instead he was on the contributors' payroll. This helps to explain the many and varied pieces of writing he did during those early days on the paper. The reasons for his not being, apparently, a full member of the staff are somewhat obscure and a little difficult to track down. It was Bartholomew who had arranged things thus, so the reason was probably to hide from his less adventurous Board the fact that he had brought in another out- sider to help his master plan of turning the paper into a viable proposition. In any event the situation did not come to the notice of John Cowley, the Chairman, until the middle of 1941 when Connor made a radio broadcast which caused consider- able controversy. Cowley summoned Connor to his office to see for himself the man who had created such a stir. Connor, for his part, thought that he had been called to receive a little praise and—hopefully—some more money, for he was not being paid much at the time. Cowley made the usual kind of formal small-talk that occurs between employer and employee, and then said that he would like to give Connor a present. Connor's imagina- tion ran riot with thoughts of crisp five pound notes when Cowley reached into his desk. But the reward was not financial; it was horticultural. Cowley solemnly handed Connor the biggest onion he had ever seen, saying 'I grew it myself'. Somewhat crestfallen and unable to say anything, Connor withdrew from the interview, onion in hand. It was not until later that he learned that the onion was Cowley's supreme accolade.

The fact that Bill Connor was technically a 'contributor' led to him being responsible for quite a number of other things besides the Cassandra column. For instance he and Bill Herbert, his friend from Arks Publicity who joined the paper in 1938, were responsible for the Live Letters page. Students of the *Mirror* speak fondly of the 'Old Codgers' and 'Lottie' and 'George, our

office lad', and sigh nostalgically at the mention of 'our trikes'.
Non-students may well be surprised to know that the page—so
ably run at present by Peter Reed—has a far greater following
than the correspondence columns in *The Times*. Indeed, when it
comes to stirring up controversy and initiating a batch of enthusiastic correspondence, a short piece in the Live Letters column
about X's soups has a much more resounding effect than the
early cuckoos and disappearance of frogs from Christ Church
Meadows so beloved by correspondents of The Thunderer.

It was during this period on Live Letters that Bill Connor and
Bill Herbert cooked up a madcap scheme typical of the mild
lunacy that affects the *Mirror* from time to time. They thought it
might be a good idea to see if it were possible to hatch out a
clutch of chicken eggs by using a human as a substitute mother.
After all, the theory was simple enough; all you had to do—so
they thought—was to keep the eggs warm, be careful not to
break them, and just wait. Through the page they managed to get
hold of a girl named Peggy who was confined to bed with a broken
leg. The eggs were entrusted to her care. For days she tended
them with the solicitous care of a mother hen. But the day never
dawned when the eggs cracked open and little fluffy yellow
chicks came chirping into the world. The suspense was enormous.
The let-down was even greater. The Old Codgers retired,
slightly puzzled at the inconsiderate behaviour of Mother Nature.

Bill Connor was also, at various times, the military correspondent of the paper, the aeronautical correspondent (a little strange
for a man who a few years before had wanted nothing more than
to join the Navy) and the cat correspondent. This latter was never
on more than an unofficial basis. He was given the assignment
because of his profound love of cats, coupled with a deep suspicion
of dogs. He was also the co-originator of a strip cartoon called
'Belinda Blue Eyes'—though, later in life, he said he wished he
had 'strangled her at birth' because she was so ineffably coy. It was
during his period as aeronautical correspondent that he helped
produce the infamous *Daily Mirror Book of Aircraft Recognition*.
This achieved a certain amount of notoriety due to the silhouette
illustrations of aircraft in it which bore a marked resemblance to
those found in *Janes' Fighting Aircraft*, a fact that the publishers of

Janes' were not slow to realize and take action on. Infringement of copyright, even in times of national emergency and for the sake of the war effort, is not permissible.

Despite all these sallies into the wilder fringes of journalism—and some of the schemes hatched at that time really appeared to be the ideas of lunatics—Bill Connor's main work was the Cassandra column. He wrote the first one within a few days of joining the *Daily Mirror* in 1935. He wrote the last one some thirty-two years later. In the years between he made many people happy—and many sad. He wrote things that people agreed with strongly. And he wrote others that people disagreed with violently. His writing was sharp as a scalpel—and blunt as a sock full of wet sand. It was hilariously funny. It was deadly serious. It was right many times—and just as often wrong. It could be amazingly clear-sighted. And it could be mulishly misguided. Looking through the book of adjectives, there are very few that could not be applied to the Cassandra column at one time or another. When it started it was insignificant. When it finished Bill Connor had carved himself a solid place in British newspaper history.

One of the questions that Bill Connor was most frequently asked during his years as a journalist was why he chose the name Cassandra. The short answer is that he did not. It was chosen for him, probably by Bartholomew. And not for particularly altruistic reasons. In later years Connor said that the reason Bartholomew had decided that he should write under a pseudonym was simply that if he (Connor) had not made a success of it, he could have been fired and replaced without the readers knowing. It was probably just as well that Connor was not aware of this at the time he accepted the job.

Cassandra was in fact only one of a number of classical noms-de-plume that were in vogue on the *Mirror* at the time. The radio correspondent (how much more elegant the title sounds than its present-day counterpart, the T.V. critic) was known as Ariel, presumably another of Bart's heavy jokes. But Cassandra? that was an odd one. In fact, when Connor was first told of the pseudonym under which he was to write, he had to look the name up. He tells the story in an article that appeared in July 1965:

I was a bit surprised to discover that I had changed my sex; was the daughter of the King of Troy; that I could foretell in the stars when the news was going to be bad; that a chap named Apollo had made many a pass at me; that nobody believed me when I spoke the unpleasant truth and that I was going to come to a sticky end by being efficiently murdered by Clytaemnestra, the wife of the mighty King Agamemnon.

So I went and had a beer to pull myself round.

The beer was obviously effective.

In these early days the Cassandra column was very much like the conjuror's rabbit; now you saw it, now you didn't. This was largely because, on some days, there was room for it and on others there was not. At that time it came under the Features Department and if they had something that was more newsworthy, then the column was left out. On average, it appeared no more than two or three times a week during the first few years. But it was during these first years that Connor began to develop his technique for writing the column. He read avidly—newspapers, books, magazines, articles, speeches, wire service reports, virtually anything that had words in it strung together into sentences. He always had a voracious appetite for the printed word. His home had rooms lined with books. In his office he was never short of reading matter. He was able to read—and digest thoroughly— —some seven or eight daily newspapers during the fifty minutes it took him to travel to the *Mirror* on the train each morning. He read at a fantastic rate. More incredibly, he was able to analyse, to group, to grade, to classify and divide all this barrage of information and hold it in his head for use at a moment's notice. Very few facts concerning the wide range of subjects he was interested in ever escaped his attention. And if one did, then it was not for long. Like every journalist he had the full resources of a highly efficient newspaper library at his disposal. He just used it a little less than most writers, or alternatively to find out information on the more abstruse facets of his subjects.

Brian Parker, a friend of his on the paper, who for a while ran the famous Pip, Squeak and Wilfred children's page, remembered Connor during this time. On the days when the column was not appearing, Parker would see him sitting quietly reading and absorbing facts. To a passer-by it might have appeared that he was simply wasting time. But he was not. It was all part of the programming of his computer mind. Nor was it just his own reading that Connor took in. Many people would pass on to him snippets, a fact here, a rumour there, an opinion somewhere else. All were duly noted. This massive armoury of facts was what, no doubt, made the words land with such striking effect on their target.

It is interesting to look back at the Cassandra columns of these first early days. Obviously they did not have the power of expression that Connor acquired as time went by. But they show that he had already developed a strong sense of outrage at injustice. Right from the start the column bears the stamp of a man who wrote about what he personally believed in. It bears the imprint of his feelings and emotions. It is personal. The columns were short and simple—and usually had a sting in the tail. This was a trick that Connor used a lot in his writing. He extended the red carpet—and then whipped it smartly away from under the feet. Here are two examples:

HELPFUL MR BROWNING

Ever heard of Mr Browning—Mr Valentine Browning? No? What a pity. He makes guns. Good guns. Smooth blue-steel guns that are straight and true. You can rely on them.

Germany relied on them to shoot Englishmen. Englishmen trusted them to shoot Germans.

Mr Browning didn't let the Germans down. And Mr Browning gave the Englishmen a fair and square deal. So Germans and Englishmen died side by side.

Do you remember Ivar Kreuger of Swedish match fame? How, when his staggering edifice of fraud began to topple he retired to the upper bedroom of an obscure flat in Paris? And how at last he shot himself and escaped from the hurricane of death and misery that his work had brought on?

Mr Browning helped him—made the neat accurate weapon with which he shot his brains out.

Now Mr Browning speaks again. Listen to his words:

'A great European war is inevitable. Munition plants are running night and day. Even then they are lagging behind orders which are coming in from many nations, including South America. 'Personally I want no war. I want no part of it. There is more money in the production of small arms in peace time than in the manufacture of munitions in time of war.'

Mr Browning, can I ask you a question? Have you a few moments to spare? Yes? Thank you.

Now take the fastest longest running jump at yourself that you can possibly manage.

Or this one:

NUMBER 89

The other day a huge flabby white-faced man sat down and wrote this letter to the publishers of a Wild West magazine called *Western Trails*.

> Alcatraz Island
> California, No. 89

Sirs: I enclose one dollar fifty cents as a year's subscription to your magazine, which I shall be obliged if you will send to the above address.—Yours faithfully . . .

The publishers of *Western Trails* got the money safely and in due course dispatched the current issue to their new subscriber in Alcatraz Island. He was pleased when he got it.

He tore the wrapper off eagerly and looked at the Contents page. Yes, it looked interesting. There were some pretty thrilling yarns. The big story was 'The Double-barrelled Decoy', followed by 'Trigger Tempest', 'Maverick Law' and 'Branded with Lead'. The drawings were good too with lots of pictures of exciting gunplay.

Then he skimmed through the advertisements. They were enthralling. If he answered them they offered to:

Teach him how to play the guitar in ten minutes;

Break him of the tobacco habit;

Reveal how to have a baby;

Show him how to be a secret service agent.

It was good, this magazine! Packed full of the right sort of reading. None of this wishy-washy stuff. He turned to the first story and was soon in the drama of 'The Double-barrelled Decoy'.

Alphonse Capone, No. 89 in the Alcatraz Penitentiary, was satisfied.

Dc

They were short, bitter-sweet columns. You didn't notice the scorpion-tail endings until they had struck home. Even in these very early days Bill Connor was writing about subjects which were to become favourite hardy perennials with him. One such subject was herrings, a childhood favourite of his. He had developed a great liking for them thanks to his Aberdonian background. They—like a lot of other food—would be described and written about in great swirls of lyrical language. His cookery columns were some of the finest pieces of descriptive writing that he ever wrote. But one column he wrote in 1935 was not quite in the usual vein.

Herrings for Breakfast

I always say there's nothing like a herring for breakfast. Some people despise 'em. Not me. Crisp and smoking hot so that the white juicy flesh comes clean away from the bone—that's the way to eat them. You can have your bacon and eggs. You can have your grilled tomatoes. But give me a herring. And they're cheap—dirt cheap. I suppose that's why some folks despise them. . . .

There are some very high cliffs on the Yorkshire coast near Bridlington called Speeton Cliffs. Yesterday the trawler 'Skegness' went ashore there. It wasn't very rough when they first went aground, so the crew waited to see if they could refloat on the rising tide. Soon it began to blow hard.

High on the cliff, exhausted coastguards peered to where the 'Skegness' was last seen. Yes, she was still there. But now she had rolled on her side. Her crew gathered in a huddled little bunch in the wheelhouse; you could just see them crouching there. Up on the cliffs they tried to fire rockets.

Seven times they shot but the line was flung back by the tearing gale. Someone signalled from the wheelhouse with a flashlamp. At 4 a.m. the flickering light stopped

There was no more wheelhouse and no more crew. Eleven men died in the thundering surf. Six widows are left.

Yes, there's nothing like herrings for breakfast—they're cheap too. Dirt cheap.

In 1936 Basil Nicholson was fired. He had been Features Editor for about eighteen months. In that time he had infuriated just about everyone he worked with. Most had quickly forgiven him

—or had been in no position to do anything about it. But Bartholomew was. And when Bart bore a grudge against someone, he usually got his revenge. Nicholson, during the short time that he was at the *Mirror*, had been an almost constant thorn in Bart's side. Bart did not understand Nicholson. He was suspicious of this witty, cynical, urbane man with the glasses and the big cigar. He found it impossible to like and to trust someone who had come from a background so totally different from his own. He may even have disliked Nicholson for his lack of experience in the harsh world of newspapers. He—Bartholomew—had worked his way up from the bottom, while Nicholson had merely drifted in by way of university and a brief spell in advertising. Bartholomew distrusted the ease of Nicholson's brilliance. Their two entirely different characters were bound to clash and grate against each other. And, since Bartholomew was in the position of greater power, it was obvious that Nicholson was the one to go.

As a farewell gesture, Cecil King gave Nicholson a trip on the maiden voyage of the 'Queen Mary'. It was a fitting present, and very much in the character of the man. Like the time when first appointed Features Editor, Nicholson had booked a room for himself for one night only at the Savoy, it was a grand symbol. It was in the same class as his walking out of his Final Examinations at Oxford, and as the cutlass which he kept on his desk when he was Features Editor. They were all absurd—but they all said: 'I am Basil Nicholson—a character. I behave as I see fit at the time. I am free to come and go as I please. You may pay me a salary, but you will never own me. I remain always myself, answerable only to me.'

It is worth considering the effect that Nicholson had on the *Mirror* during his brief stay there. For he had a very great impact on the paper, and one that has been underestimated. He was hired originally because of his knowledge of strip cartoon techniques; the Mirror, thirty-two years after his departure, still runs the equivalent of a half-page of strip cartoons, as well as a further section of ordinary cartoons. One of Nicholson's early and short-lived ideas had been a gossip column. It ran for only a few issues and was brought to a sudden halt after some disparaging remarks about Charles Laughton's wife Elsa Lanchester had appeared in the paper. Laughton was infuriated. He went round to the offices of the *Mirror* and threatened to punch the writer on the nose and to sue the paper as well. Today the 'Inside Page' of the Mirror is a little less scandalous, but is a gossip column nonetheless. Nicholson also probably suggested having a regular columnist, as opposed to a varied selection of anonymous correspondents. Without Nicholson there may well have never been a Cassandra or a Donald Zec or a Marjorie Proops or a Noel Whitcomb or a Rex North in either the *Daily* or *Sunday Mirrors*. Nicholson also felt very strongly—as did Bartholomew—about the use of large-space pictures in the paper. Indeed, on one occasion, when Bill Connor had written an article that was under length, Nicholson had said: 'Don't bother to write more—we'll use a bloody great picture to fill the gap.' Bart had been furious, but had not prevented it. The two of them caught on to the adage of a picture being worth a thousand words a great deal sooner than others in Fleet Street. And the *Mirror* has always been, since the days of the tabloid revolution, a paper that uses and understands pictures better than anyone.

It would be a little naïve, however, to pretend that all these ideas were carefully thought out and examined in detail, dissected and analysed. Nicholson's technique was very much that of saying: 'What if we did this ... or that?', either to the right people or alternatively to no one and simply going ahead with it. He was a man of instinct. Ideas felt right to him. Sometimes they were wrong—very wrong. But the proof of the rightness of his instinct is that many of his best ideas still exist today.

If Nicholson was able to make the mark that he did on the *Daily Mirror* in just two short years, one wonders what he might have been capable of doing had he stayed longer. If he had not been quite so self-destructive, he may well have become one of the great giants of the newspaper industry.

One thing further must be said about Nicholson; he felt no grudge against Bart or the *Mirror* for firing him. Indeed he may have been totally unaware of the impact he made on the paper. To him it was a job that allowed him a little more leeway to carry out his great—and often crazy—schemes; schemes that he hoped would bring him both money and satisfaction. It did not work out—so he left for other pastures. But the signature, however faint, is still there after thirty-odd years.

If Bill Connor felt a gap in his circle of friends at the *Mirror* after Basil Nicholson's departure, it did not last for long. New friends were joining the paper, and in any case he was busy studying and visiting pre-war Germany. In 1933, while Bill Connor was writing advertising for Harpic and Black Magic at J. Walter Thompson, Hitler became Chancellor. When Connor first joined the *Daily Mirror* in 1935, Hitler was testing out his air force and his army under the guise of helping Franco in the Spanish Civil War. Two years later he had joined in an unholy alliance with Mussolini. People were beginning to talk about the probability of war instead of the possibility. Bill Connor, like many other young men of the time, realized that he was going to be involved in this war—the second one in his lifetime. He viewed the events in Europe with the deeper interest of the newspaper man. Horrible though they were, they had to be reported. And condemned.

During his first four years with the *Mirror*, Bill Connor went to Germany a great number of times. He viewed it on two very separate planes. The country he liked very much—he spent one holiday walking down the Rhine with friends. The Nazis he loathed with a deep and complete hatred. He observed them on his visits to Germany. He went to their great rallies. He watched the strutting Führer, like some demented peacock, at official celebrations. He saw it all with the horrified fascination of a man who watches an apple being turned rotten by the maggot inside it. And he wrote about it. Not just the almost weekly diatribes against Hitler and his cronies, but also little bitter pieces about the effect that the super-patriotic lunatic was having on the German people and their country. One such was a short column about the German racing car driver Hans Stuck. It was called 'The Crown of Thorns'.

Fair-haired Hans Stuck drives a German racing car. And he drives it fast. Probably there are only about three people alive who can drive a car faster and more skilfully. He was the idol of German racing crowds. People leapt on their seats and cheered themselves hoarse as he flashed by in the International Grand Prix.

Then something happened. He married. Married a Jewess. Forgot all that Hitler had said about non-Aryans and went ahead and married the girl he loved.

Three days ago he entered a German race—a long twisting course up the side of a mountain. He climbed into his car. With a shattering roar the long white Auto-Union rocketed into the bends. Nailed to a tree, a poster caught his eye:

'Spit on him—Hans Stuck, the husband of a Jewess!' Hans stood on everything.

Near the winning line a banner was stretched across the road. On it roared the words: 'Stuck—Traitor to Hitler'. He passed the post and they told him he had won. All records were broken.

Four minutes later they gave him First Prize—a framed and signed portrait of Adolf Hitler.

Not unnaturally the German masters got a little annoyed with this foreign journalist who lashed them so relentlessly. He was arrested and held for a number of hours by the Gestapo during his last visit less than a month before the outbreak of war. It was a warning to him. After the war he discovered that his name had been placed on the notorious Nazi Black List of people who were to be shot by the Germans after their invasion of England. He was suitably gratified that he had managed to annoy them that much.

CHAPTER FOUR

YOUNG MAN WITH A
SPORTS CAR

GETTING inside the mind of a man, to discover his feelings, his beliefs, his fears, his hopes is as difficult as getting a camel through the eye of a needle. Friends and contemporaries can each supply one or two pieces of a very complex jigsaw; collect together enough of these pieces and there emerges a rough but nevertheless incomplete picture. Some men keep diaries in which they record their inmost thoughts. Bill Connor was not one of these, either through introspection or idleness or simply because he spent most of his time writing for a living and could not therefore be bothered with them. However, from two pieces of his writing it is possible to get an insight into Connor during the 1930s. Both were articles that he wrote for the *Daily Mirror* shortly before he joined it in 1935. The first, entitled 'I am a young man of 25', is printed in full below.

I am 25 years old and a bachelor. I earn ten pounds a week. When I say *earn* that is only relatively true. I am paid ten pounds every week because I put up an appearance of working which is as good— if not slightly better—than most of the people who are employed with me. Compared with the work done and money earned by the majority of people I meet, I am well paid.

For instance my charlady. She keeps my hundred-pound-a-year flat clean and tidy. She washes my dishes, makes my bed, dusts, buys my shopping and lights my fires. She gets ten shillings every Friday for this job which takes her about fifteen hours a week. Work to me is the amount of effort required to do the things I dislike doing. Few people can like washing other people's dishes and cleaning other people's fireplaces. For this my charlady gets 8*d* an hour. I suppose I spend about 4 hours a day doing work—a total of 22 hours a week. For this I get 9/1*d*. an hour. I must be lucky.

I am interested in money, cars and women—not necessarily in that order. I want to earn much more money than I do at present—how much I am not sure for I have noticed that as my salary has increased from about one pound to ten pounds a week I am still in the same position of having neither change in my pocket nor money in the bank.

I have recently kept a record of how I spend my money.

Here is an actual budget for one week:

	£	s	d
Rent	£2	0	0
Cleaning		10	0
Laundry		3	6
Dinners		15	0
Lunches		12	0
Drink	1	8	6
Food for flat (Breakfasts, etc.)		7	6
Newspapers		2	3
Income Tax		16	0
Petrol and oil for car		16	6
	£7	11	3

Balance £2 8s 9d—from which must come Light, Gas, Clothes and Life Insurance.

There's not much to show for this. Food, drink and transport account for 40%—a very high figure.

There's no money left over for buying anything that will not be consumed immediately. It seems to be almost the ideal 'hand-to-mouth' budget. The figure for drink looks high. Do other people spend like this?

When I read the newspapers I see more and more war talk. War is intensely interesting because it involves *me*. The idea of war is a familiar one. I was just old enough to remember the outbreak of the last war. I remember the food queues, and the dried eggs you got. I remember the air raids and how they sang God Save the King when a Zeppelin came down in flames. I have never fought but I have been brought up reading war books, seeing war films, hearing war talk. If war is declared and conscription is started I shall be one of the first to be embroiled. I shan't like this much because statesmen and military experts of unquestionable integrity have assured me that it is quite likely that I shall be shot, gassed, bombed, burnt, poisoned, infected with disease or shattered into a living wreck within a short space of time. I like my country and I like my countrymen. I neither like nor dislike foreigners. They don't directly concern me. I should hate to fight against them because it would be dangerous to me and a gross waste of my time.

Women concern me a great deal. More than I wish. I want them—but I rarely like them. They take too much for granted. I am continually extricating myself from circumstances that I have not created. Before I know where I am, I am involved. Curiosity more than anything else leads me on. I take a girl out to lunch. All very fine. Next to a theatre perhaps. Still all very fine. We make another date—out somewhere in the car. Bit of change this time—faint but discernible; I am being watched. A few rapid calculations are being made—the skeleton of a plan is being formed. There's nothing cold-blooded about this—I find girls generally can't help doing this even when they aren't really interested. I let things go a bit further. Now for some technique.

How well I know the symptoms. Often it's the possessive stuff. 'We'll go there together' (the blazes we will!). Or the clinging method, 'I simply can't go without you—you *must* come along' (oh yeah?). Or the take-it-for-granted style, 'Yes I said you'd be along—I meant to tell you the other night' (nice of you!). These are ominous signs. I feel I am being quietly invited by a sweet little girl to the top of a large flight of stairs that are in total darkness. The top stairs have been well greased. Half way down three steps are missing. I am about to be gently pushed at the top stair.... When I recover consciousness I shall be married. It's not that I am unduly cautious. It's just the plain simple fact that one is nervous about being inveigled or persuaded in any way into the most binding contract to which it is possible to be a partner. I may be married some day but I do reserve the right to pick my choice and have my fancy.

The second one was called 'Did I ever tell you about my operation?'

Two professional-looking butchers softly appear. They are wearing white smocks and on their heads they have white caps rather like those that the American sailors wear. They are pushing a trolley that runs on big tyred wheels—a refined tumbril affair covered with huge rubber hot water bottles. I look at their faces with interest. They have no expression and they are stupid. They lift me from my bed with gentleness and care. My mouth is dry. On a dirty piece of yellow paper I have agreed with hospital authorities that I am willing and eager for my operation. Also I have assured them that I have no false teeth to swallow nor a glass eye to lose. As I am wheeled on the trolley through the long ward, I reflect on the events of the past few hours.

*　　*　　*

First, there was the lay preacher; a serious, studious man, who went straight to the point.

'Do you believe in God?'

ME: 'No.'

LAY PREACHER: 'How old are you?'

ME: 'Twenty eight.'

L.P.: 'You are young, my son.'

ME: 'Twenty eight.'

L.P.: 'Are you afraid of this operation?'

ME: 'Yes.'

L.P.: 'God is Love!'

Silence.

L.P.: 'GOD IS LOVE!'

We parted politely, but with feelings of deep suspicion. A decent space of time was allowed to pass before a black-robed priest appeared, young, athletic and pink. His visit was timed better. The psychology of the Catholic Church has never been anything but perfect. Zero hour was near. He was smiling, looking extremely friendly, and said—

'Good morning.'

ME: 'Good morning.'

P.: 'I think I can help you.'

ME: 'You remind me of a buzzard.'

P.: 'Why?'

ME: 'The buffalo when he has strayed from the herd and is lost usually dies of thirst. For some hours before he stumbles for the last time a black speck has been hovering high in the air above him. Soon the first buzzard is joined by others—a wheeling black squadron that is soon to settle on the dying beast.'

P.: 'Rather a good metaphor. Untrue of course.'

ME: 'Thank you.'

P.: 'My only wish is to help you.'

ME: 'You are too late for I have every hope of being dead by half past three this afternoon.'

P.: 'What utter rot you do talk. I am going to give you my blessing.'

ME: 'Proceed.'

The trolley arrives at a lift shaft. There is no pillow under my head and I am staring straight up. We trundle into the lift and I look at a distant skylight far above. It grows bigger as we go up and we arrive at the top landing.

All is bright and beautiful. White floors, high ceilings, enormous windows. It's warm, too. The sweet smell of ether makes me feel sick. A young man, who, at first, because of his white overall, mask and cap, I do not recognize, comes across to me. He speaks first. 'You here too?'

ME: "Fraid so.' (I just remember that he is the student who has talked to me in the wards.)

YOUNG STUDENT: 'You don't want to get the wind up, you know.'

ME: 'Oh, I'm fine.'

Y.S.: 'I probably feel much worse than you do.'

ME: 'Why is that?'

Y.S.: 'Fearful hangover—drunk as a newt last night!'

ME: 'Oh, tough luck . . .'

And so it goes on. The crashingly awful fool blethers away telling me about his ridiculous and squalid boozing the night before. How he and eight of his silly friends got into a taxi.

I gather that I am a little early, and that I must wait for five minutes until the previous operation is finished. The dreary fatuous voice in my ear drones on '. . . and so I said to the policeman, "Look here, Robert, you can't do that. . . ."'

I wonder whether to stop him. I decide not to. I have a lot to be thankful for.

There are several thousand people in this country who commit suicide. Most of them have got the bother of ovens, disinfectants and knives to consider, whereas it's almost certain that some of the most distinguished medical skill in the country will do the job for me. And painlessly too. That's very important.

Quite dispassionately I have worked out my wish for death. The logic of it all surprised me.

What do I live for? Enjoyment, What are the main sources of enjoyment for an ordinary young man? Money, women and friends. I have a little money. It brings me the ordinary things—good food, a car, entertainments and a certain amount of travel. I do not desire much more.

Women are more difficult. They are fine creatures. Of most of them you can say that the more you know them the more you like them. Until you get to a certain point, and, if you're quick, you can see the octopus in them. They want *you*.

Often they don't care about your possessions or your work. They want the *true and secret you*; the little fellow deep down inside who gets frightened and helps you to tell lies; who boasts, and who admires you. Give them this, and you are done.

Friends can be worth a lot. Given sufficient number no one need be coroner's meat.

* * *

Now the time has come, I look at the clock with a strange feeling— twenty-six minutes past three. A man puts a cotton wool pad over my face. 'Breathe slowly and count twenty.' Nothing seems to happen. Then a faint prickling at the back of the brain.

Then it's like breathing hot, dry air that scorches you deep down.

Now I can hear my heart far, far off. It grows louder quickly. Lights burst and blaze before my eyes. I try to shut them. I can't. My head is in a vice and my jaw is being slowly forced up into the roof of my mouth. . . .

* * *

My Irish priest friend visited me a lot afterwards. He'd read the newspapers to me, quickly get tired of it and start long-winded arguments about wanting to be dead.

YOUNG PRIEST: 'The doctors saved you and did you a good turn— they didn't swindle you.'

ME: 'All right. Then have it your own way. Can you read fortunes?'

Y.P.: 'No.'

ME: 'Look at my hand. This is the life-line. Now compare it with yours. It's only about two-thirds of the length.'

Y.P.: 'Well, what does that mean?'

ME: 'It means I shall escape you, for I shall die young. Will you come and mourn me when they've patted me on the face with a burial spade and the daisies start to grow?'

Y.P.: 'Certainly not!'

ME: 'Why not?'

Y.P.: 'You will be in the hands of our Head Office—and they are not so patient as I am.'

These articles, as well as showing a few of Connor's early beliefs, have an amusing story to them. They were two of three articles commissioned from Connor by Basil Nicholson who was by then the Features Editor of the *Daily Mirror*. Connor was going through a sticky patch at J. Walter Thompson; it was during the period he was thinking of joining the *Mirror* and JWT were thinking of firing him. The articles appeared in the newspaper without any name on them but the day the first was published it was spotted by Sandy Mackendrick, the film director, who was working as an artist at JWT, and he cut it out and left it on Connor's desk with a note saying what a fine piece of writing he thought it was. Connor, seeing Mackendrick's note, firmly denied authorship of the piece. A couple of weeks later another article that he had written for Nicholson appeared. Again Mackendrick cut it out and left it on Connor's desk with a similar note to the first. Connor denied authorship of it even more firmly than he had the first. The third article, still anonymous, appeared a couple of weeks later. This time Mackendrick cut it out and left it on the desk—but without a note. He saw Connor a couple of times that day and still said nothing about the piece. The suspense built up until finally Connor went into Sandy Mackendrick's room and said, 'What's the matter? Wasn't the bloody piece as good as the other two?'

Throughout his life Bill Connor had—somewhat surprisingly for a man who knew, and was known by, hundreds of people—a very small group of close friends. And most of them date from the time he first had a flat, with one or two going as far back as schooldays. There was Tubby Belcher, the 'massive brain', who had worked with him at Arks Publicity, then spent a year with Arks in Ireland, and was, by the mid-30s, back and looking for a job and a place to live; there was Terence Wright, who had been an account executive at Arks; Bill Herbert—now Cartoon Features Editor of the *Daily Mirror*—another ex-Arks friend. Into this group one day in 1934 came the man who was to be the most riotous and delightfully uncontrollable member of their clan— Dick Lind. Lind was a German, whose father owned a battery-making company, and he was living and working in England as the personal assistant to the managing director of Britannia

Batteries in Redditch, a subsidiary company of his father's concern. Connor's first meeting with Lind was at a party given by John Craddock, another friend of his, who at that time worked for Britannia Batteries. He was brought to the party by Terence Wright, who knew him as a business contact. The meeting was not an auspicious one. Lind had that very day smashed up his Bugatti and was bemoaning the fact in an over-loud voice. Connor—never one to suffer extroverts for long—made it quite clear to his friends that he disliked 'that noisy fool' and then proceeded to have a huge argument with him. Somehow it progressed no further, and when they met again shortly afterwards, it was as if for the first time. They got along with one another marvellously. It was the beginning of a very stimulating friendship, one that was to last right up until the war when Lind died.

Lind introduced Connor and his group of friends to all kinds of new and exciting pleasures. Like motor-racing, for example. He himself had a succession of Bugattis which he used to race from time to time at places such as Shelsey Walsh, and his enthusiasm infected them all. On one celebrated occasion Connor managed to get one press ticket to a certain race meeting—which was annoying, since there were about six of them who wanted to go and could not really afford to pay the entrance fee. Lind solved the problem by borrowing a large open Alvis from a friend, probably without the friend's permission, since this was very much in character. They all piled in and crouched on the floor and the tonneau cover was fixed in position over them. Connor drove and was able to show his pass and sweep straight through. He quickly found a quiet spot, opened up the tonneau, and out poured the rest of the party.

Lind was a great aficionado of the night club scene. He knew them all—and had been thrown out of most of them. Once he and Mick Connor, after spending an evening in their favourite one, decided that they did not want to walk home. The problem was that it was far too late for buses and they did not have the price of a taxi between them. They were both somewhat worse for the champagne that was always Lind's favourite drink, and when he said to Mick Connor, 'We shall ride home in style—get into that Rolls Royce and drive,' Mick was not the one to disagree. They managed to get to the bottom end of Bond Street, with the owner and other passers-by in full pursuit, before they crashed into a shop window. The rest of the night was spent in Brixton Jail, and the following morning Bill Connor had to come around with the week's housekeeping money and bail them out.

On another occasion Lind's formidable thirst came in very handy. He had just been on a business trip to Paris and Bill Connor had agreed to meet him at the airport on his return. As Lind was passing through Customs, the officer asked him if he had anything to declare. 'Nothing, save these two bottles of brandy which I have purchased for medicinal purposes,' said Lind. The Customs Officer protested at this, informing Lind that he would have to pay duty on the brandy. Lind said that he had no intention of paying duty. The Customs man said that in that case he would have to impound the brandy. Lind, with a typically extravagant gesture, grabbed one of the bottles and drank the entire contents. Within a matter of minutes he had passed out cold. Bill Connor was faced with the unenviable task of taking him home. The next day, when Lind had regained consciousness, he said with great glee, 'Well, I got one of them through without having to pay duty!'

During this period Bill Connor had a number of flats, all with a common oasis-like quality. This was primarily because, whilst he had a steady job, few of his friends had. As a result the flats always had a floating population. There were never less than three inhabitants—and usually there were more. He often complained that they were using his flats as high-class doss-houses. In addition to acquiring all sorts of tenants, his flats also acquired a number of somewhat peculiar fittings. One of them—of which he was inordinately proud—was an astronomical telescope which his father had given to him. It was a very large brass affair and was always trained on the clock tower at St Pancras Station which could be seen over the rooftops from the flat at Tavistock Mansions in Herbrand Street. And the reason that the telescope was pointed at the clock tower was very simple; neither Connor nor any of his friends at that time owned a watch. So, if they wanted to know the time, all they had to do was take a peek through the telescope. And it worked just as well after dark since the people at St Pancras were kind enough to have the clock illuminated at night.

Another less useful object that Connor acquired in a later flat was a full-size concert grand piano. He was then living in a modest mews flat just off Regent's Park. The furniture was mainly conspicuous by its absence. The lino was full of holes, some of them covered by mattresses which served as beds at night and as couches by day. As a crowning touch, the roof leaked. And when it rained there would be a mad scramble for buckets and sauce-pans and a massive tarpaulin. The buckets were to catch as much rain as possible so that it did not soak into the already-decaying floorboards; the tarpaulin, instead of being used to keep the occupants of the flat dry, was put over the piano to protect it. Considering that the piano was daily subjected to musical attack by some of the most inept pianists of the time, it seemed a rather strange order of priorities. Connor himself was one of the perpetrators of this musical mayhem. He had, as a child, learnt to play the piano—or rather, had been more or less forced to by his very musical father. In later life he rejoiced in the self-awarded title of 'world's worst piano player'. That this title was fully justified was usually proved at Christmas. Some friends of his held a Christmas party every year, at which Paddy Roberts, the song writer, was a regular guest. As the party wore on—and after a suitable amount of beer and bullying—Connor and Paddy Roberts would take to the keyboard to play a fearsome duet version of 'Frankie and Johnnie'. Roberts would play simply and effectively; Connor on the other hand, in the way that only bad pianists can, would attempt all kinds of musical trickery, modula-tions, key changes, rhythm changes, all of them uniformly awful. On one well-remembered occasion, Paddy Roberts, at once suffering and enjoying it all, suddenly cried out, at a par-ticularly tortured passage, 'For God's sake, Bill, change gear. You'll kill us both!' It was perhaps lucky for all concerned that Connor only chose to play the piano once a year.

In August 1934 Terence Wright was having trouble with his girl friend's sister. She had no boy friend of her own and tagged along with the two of them as an unwanted chaperone. In an effort to get her out of the way, Wright decided to find a boy friend for her. So he asked a close friend of his to meet them in Redditch for a foursome one week-end. Then, at the last moment, the friend cried off. Wright was sitting in a pub at lunchtime with the two girls when in walked Bill Connor, who had driven up to Redditch on the off-chance of meeting Terence. Wright was saved at the last moment. He went off with his girl friend and left Bill Connor with the sister. Her name was Mair Morgan. She was eighteen.

Mair Morgan was, like Connor, a twin. Her father, Robert Morgan, a Welshman, was French master at a school in Redditch. Their mother had died of T.B. when the girls were only fourteen and they had been brought up by their father. At first she was not over-impressed by the thin man with big glasses who had turned up unexpectedly; but she did like his smart green M.G. sports car. 'I fell in love with the car first, then with its owner.' She was at the time a very keen hockey player and had in fact had a trial for the county team. She also was, as she still is, fanatically keen on Shakespeare. She and her sister often cycled from Redditch to Stratford-on-Avon to visit the theatre. Neither of these interests was appreciated by Connor. Writing to her a few days after their first meeting he said how nice it had been to meet her and that she 'should grow your fringe a little longer, give up playing hockey and concentrate a little less on William Shakespeare and a little more on William Connor'.

Bill Connor's courtship of Mair Morgan was a long one. Most week-ends he would drive up to Redditch from London to see her. They would then go off around the countryside, sometimes to quiet pubs, sometimes to watch motor-racing or hill-climbs (Shelsey Walsh was a great favourite of theirs).

Gradually his reserve towards women was broken down. Mair Morgan was not the single-minded, grab-your-man-quick type of girl he had written so caustically about. He found that he was able to relax and enjoy her company. She may well have fallen in love with him soon after they first met; he seemed rather to drift into love, with no conscious effort and no last-ditch resistance to preserve his bachelorhood.

They were married at Paddington Registry Office on
Ec

2 December 1938. Norah Connor, his sister, remembers the slightly off-hand invitation she received to the wedding. Bill Connor said 'Oh, by the way, I'm getting married next week. Would you like to come?' Since, over the years, she had become used to being introduced to various girls not by their names, but by the simple sobriquet of 'the girl friend', she was not absolutely sure which one it was that Bill Connor was going to marry. She was relieved and delighted to find that it was Mair Morgan.

For nearly a year after their marriage, Bill and Mair Connor lived in a flat in Fitzjohn's Avenue in Hampstead. Then, after seeing a house they liked in the country, not far from where his parents were living, they moved to a village called Skirmett, about seven miles from Henley-on-Thames, in the Hambleden Valley. Their new home was an old brick and flint house called the Old Forge. It was a lot further for Bill Connor to travel to his work, but they both loved the country too much for this to be anything but a minor consideration.

Most week-ends would find them entertaining a houseful of their friends. Philip Zec, Bill Herbert, Dick Lind, Terence Wright and a whole host of others would be in and out of the house at all times.

It was during these early days in the Buckinghamshire countryside that Bill Connor really got to know the local people, their habits and their customs. Anyone who has ever moved into a close-knit country community like a village will have experienced for himself how easy it is to be made to feel like a foreigner, and how difficult it can be to become readily accepted by the local people.

The Connors found this at first. But Bill Connor had made, during week-ends spent with his parents at Lane End, three miles from their own home, a useful ally and a lifelong friend in Len Wise.

Len Wise is a short man who, until recent years, was also a very round man. At his prime he weighed in at over twenty stone. He is also an intensely amiable man. He wears a smile the whole day long and it is very doubtful whether he has ever shown so much as a hint of ill-temper towards anyone. He knew—and was liked by—most of the people in the area. He soon became a bosom companion of the Connors and their friends.

One story about him illustrates just how much of a countryman he is. When he and Bill Connor first met, Wise was working as bus driver with the local bus company. His conductor—who also became a close friend of the Connors—was a man named Maurice Hawes. One of their bus routes took them past a field that was, for a large part of the year, virtually bursting with pheasants. They strutted around arrogantly, confident that since they were on private land, they were safe—at least until the official time for pheasant shooting came around. But they had not reckoned with Wise and Hawes. Both of them liked a bit of plump pheasant to eat and so they hit on a simple scheme. Hawes carried a shotgun in the luggage rack of the bus. When they drove past the field and spotted a particularly inviting bird, Hawes would ring the bell to stop the bus, nip out with his shotgun and return a few minutes later with a delicious trophy. Then they would carry on with the more mundane business of running a bus service.

Despite his being a close friend of Bill Connor, Len Wise could not resist an impish urge from time to time. One such occasion was at Freddie Cutler's pub. One of the locals who drank there was a man named Hedgington who rode a tricycle and was renowned and respected for his evil temper. Connor, at that time, knew very little about him and when one day he saw the trike outside he asked Wise to whom it belonged. Wise told him casually and said why didn't Bill Connor take a ride on it? Old Hedgington wouldn't mind. So Connor climbed aboard and gaily rode around for a few minutes. As he returned, the owner came out. All hell broke loose. Connor was extremely embarrassed. And Len Wise's little joke succeeded beyond all expectation.

When war broke out on 3 September 1939, life for Bill Connor and his wife was not immediately affected, other than the worry that everyone shared about what was going to happen to them. Being a journalist, he was in a reserved occupation. He was also now aged thirty, and was therefore fairly low down in the order of call-up. As in other wars, it was the younger men who were being taken first as cannon-fodder.

He did, however, join the Home Guard. Along with most of his local friends he became a member of 'E' Battalion, Fourth

Bucks Home Guard. Like most of the Home Guard units during those early days of the war they were a pretty ramshackle lot. For a while their most lethal weapons were pick-handles liberally decorated with barbed wire, and an airgun that might have caused discomfort to an incautious sparrow but was little match for a determined German paratrooper. But the spirit of camaraderie was high. Small patrols would spend long hours stumbling around the beech woods that abound in the Chilterns—long hours made longer by the number of times they managed to lose themselves either in the woods or in public bars that they just happened upon.

It was an uneasy time for the country, and for Bill Connor. He and the *Mirror* daily irritated the War Cabinet with their editorial arrows in an attempt to burst the balloon of complacency that seemed to envelop them. He was also writing his first book, *The English at War*, which was published in 1941. It was a short treatise on how various sectors such as the Church, the City and the Common People of Britain react in a wartime situation. It was a barbed little booklet, in typical Cassandra style. This is the foreword he wrote for it:

> The Generals die in their beds. The Politicians catch the last aeroplane away from the Fatherland. The Kings escape over frontiers to raise toy courts in countries where they are barely tolerated. The Great Merchants disappear from the market-place to hurl defiance from some foreign bourse.
>
> Only the Common People remain.
>
> In defeat the ordinary people pay the price. They foot the blood-soaked bill.
>
> In victory they get a little pomp, a brief burst of cheering, a brave array of talk, perhaps even a little glow of pride mixed with the bitter memory of sons and lovers who will never return. The loot they never see. The ships, the guns, the tanks and the planes that change hands are pawns—remote and meaningless. The mines, the blast furnaces and the armament works that are part of the reparation mean nothing to them. The vast territories and the new frontiers are coloured marks on a map that doesn't interest them. The dividends of victorious war are to them little more than ashes sweetened with a little cheap scent.
>
> But in the waging of war, it is the Common People who fight,

who slave, who drown, who are burnt, who are mutilated, who are entombed and who bear the fierce unremitting yoke of pain and tears.

The Common People! Rich as well as poor. Equal in goodness of heart towards mankind. Kind and foolish. Tender and sad. Gentle and simple. Enduring and patient. Theirs is the courage that remains unstained in the engulfing smear of treachery, hate and revenge.

God must like the Common People. He made them mad and bad, wise and foolish. He even made them funny so that He could laugh at and with them.

But most of the time He made them good.

So God created man in His own image, in the image of God created He him.

This chilling and frighteningly true prophecy was written in the early days of the biggest bloodbath in history, and some time before its full horrors were realized. Had Harry Guy Bartholomew realized quite how much his private joke of giving Bill Connor the pseudonym 'Cassandra' would rebound in his face, he might have had second thoughts.

CHAPTER FIVE

THE PEN AND THE SWORD

THE *Daily Mirror* has always had something in common with Jehovah's Witnesses, the Noise Abatement Society and the Society for Distressed Gentlefolk; they all have a great crusading spirit. Indeed, it is the crusades that have long been an integral and highly important part of the *Mirror*. Some have been laughable. And others serious. They have been parodied and they have been praised. There have been good crusades, with laudable results. And there have been bad ones, too. But never was there a more important crusade than when the *Mirror* took on the Government at the beginning of the Second World War.

In simple terms the *Daily Mirror* did not like Chamberlain. In fact, two men on the *Mirror* detested him. They were Richard Jennings, who was the great leader writer for the newspaper in the late 1930s and early 1940s and Bill Connor. When Chamberlain returned from Munich, the *Mirror*'s editorial was one of the harshest in its criticism. During the ominous lull of the next twelve months the *Mirror* kept up its attack. Hardly a week went by without its throwing a few more journalistic darts in an effort to shake the Government out of its lethargy. The *Mirror*'s attitude was a simple one. It knew that there was going to be a war. The country knew that there was going to be a war. But did the Government? From their actions it appeared not; and hence the constant goading and prodding from the *Mirror*. It demanded that measures be taken to prepare the country for the inevitable war. It said that most of the Cabinet were too incompetent or too obstinate to remain. Most of all it criticized Chamberlain's ineffectual leadership. It deplored the fact that Churchill was not made a member of the War Cabinet until almost too late in the day. And when Churchill was finally invited to join the Cabinet and accepted, it still accused the Cabinet of being too old and having too much dead wood in it.

The war for the *Daily Mirror* started on 3 September 1939.

That morning its front page carried a picture of a lion's head—the symbol of the British fighting spirit. Three days later the *Mirror* fired the first of its wartime barrages. Bill Connor's article took the form of a whole page mocked up to look like a 'Wanted' poster:

WANTED—FOR MURDER . . . FOR KIDNAPPING . . . FOR THEFT
AND FOR ARSON

Adolf Hitler, alias Adolf Schickelgruber, Adolf Hittler or Hidler. Last heard of in Berlin, September 3rd 1939. Aged 50, high 5ft. 8½ins., dark hair, frequently brushes one lock over left forehead. Blue eyes. Sallow complexion, stout build, weight about 11st. 3lb. Suffers from acute monomania, with periodic fits of melancholia. Frequently bursts into tears when crossed. Harsh guttural voice, and has a habit of raising right hand to shoulder level. DANGEROUS!'

Long before the war the *Daily Mirror*'s masters had realized that they controlled a very important medium. It was read avidly by 'the people'—the factory workers, the shop-assistants, the housewives, the butchers, the bakers, and the candlestick makers. There were millions of them. And the *Mirror* was their paper. It talked their language. It was never condescending towards them. It was on their side, against the 'Them' of the upper classes. It was the barometer of their feelings. With this in mind, the policy of the *Mirror* in the early days of the war was a simple one—to help get things moving. And to act as a public watchdog.

This the *Mirror* did admirably. It seized hold of any of the numerous examples of Government muddling and dealt the offenders a severe bite in the rump of their self-satisfaction. Bill Connor's particular target during this time was the stupidity and inflexibility of some of the military thinkers. He fulminated against the order that forbade serving men from walking arm-in-arm with their girl friends. He took up his writing cudgels to deliver a hefty thump to the minds who had decided that it was more important that the Home Guard should be equipped with regulation ties than that they should be supplied with rifles and ammunition. He deplored the bull, the button polishing and the drill, in language that the soldiers loved and the senior officers detested. And when Connor was short of military targets there were always plenty of civilian ones. During the dark days of 1940, when an invasion by the Germans looked very possible, a lot of people fled to America to keep their skins intact. Connor hit out at them with an article headed 'The Dermatologists'. Each time he found a new piece of ineptitude he dealt with it with all the gentleness of a ten-inch piece of lead piping being applied with some considerable energy to the skull.

For the first fifteen months or so of the war, the Government endured most of the barbs. They were certainly stung by them—and in many cases took corrective measures—but they gritted their teeth and carried on. The war still had to be fought, the country had to be roused and encouraged during the early months when defeat looked possible. But in January 1941 things suddenly changed. Churchill made the first warning noises. In a letter he wrote to Cecil King, he made his disapproval of the *Mirror*'s wartime policy very clear. He objected in particular to two pieces that Bill Connor had written. The first was about a story, attributed to the American magazine *Life*, concerning a report that Anthony Eden, the War Minister, had written to Churchill about the situation in the Near East. Churchill was supposed to have returned it with a succinct note attached which said: 'As far as I can see you have used every cliché except "God is love" and "Please adjust your dress before leaving"!' The second article that Churchill complained about was one which said that some Cabinet ministers appeared to be engaged in a game of musical chairs with one another's jobs. It ended by saying: 'The trouble with this particular game is that it is being played to a funeral march. Ours.'

Cecil King replied to Churchill pointing out that the *Mirror*'s attitude was not one of personal criticism of him or Anthony Eden. It was directed towards some of the other less able ministers and, more importantly, to the fact that the nation's war effort was not as good as it might be. Churchill was obviously annoyed by this letter. He wrote again to King and in his letter likened the *Mirror*'s effort to those of a Fifth Column.

The correspondence began to hot up. Churchill scored a good point when he took up a reference that King had made describing

Bill Connor's writing as 'hard-hitting' and 'vitriolic' in one of his previous letters. He pointed out that vitriol throwing was thought to be one of the worst of crimes. By the end of February, however, the correspondence had cooled down. An uneasy truce was tacitly declared. Churchill had made his mind known. The *Mirror* had been dealt a sharp Prime Ministerial rap over the knuckles. It had been told to be a good boy.

There now enters another actor in this drama—Herbert Morrison, Home Secretary in the wartime Cabinet. It is important to remember that Morrison had been a contributor to the *Mirror* in the immediate pre-war period, and had written a series of fortnightly articles for the paper.

Bill Connor attacked Morrison in a number of articles. In particular he criticized Morrison for closing the *Daily Worker*. He asked what sense there was in doing this since the Russians had by then joined the Allies. He also referred to Morrison as 'the well-known chief censor and public turnkey'. The Home Secretary was very angry and Connor found he had made an enemy for himself. It was not long before his enemy had the opportunity of exacting his revenge.

It happened over a cartoon by Philip Zec that appeared on 3 March 1942. It was one of a series which had been designed specifically to shock people into being less wasteful. It showed a shipwrecked sailor clinging to a life-raft, with the seas raging about him—a grim reminder that the German U-boats were sinking a great deal of shipping in the Atlantic. Zec had originally captioned the cartoon: 'Petrol is dearer now'—a reference to the fact that sailors were risking their lives time and time again and not to the fact that the Government had just increased the price of petrol. Bill Connor, who was sharing an office with Zec, saw and liked the cartoon immensely—except for the caption. He thought it needed more impact. And so he suggested the caption which was to get him and the *Mirror* into a great deal of trouble. He said it ought to read: 'The price of petrol has been raised by a penny (Official).'

Most people who saw the cartoon got from it the meaning that had been intended—that they should be less wasteful. Garages all over the country asked for enlarged copies so that they could shame people into saving as much petrol as possible. Hundreds of people wrote to the *Mirror* saying that, as a direct result of seeing the cartoon, they had put their cars away for the duration.

There were a few, however, who read a different meaning into it. And Herbert Morrison was one. He said: 'To me—I may be dull, narrow-minded and unimaginative—the cartoon meant that the seaman struggling on the raft at sea—alone, almost exhausted —was risking his life in order that somebody might get additional profits. It was a wicked cartoon.' There were others in the Government who agreed with his interpretation—Ernest Bevin, the Minister of Labour, and the Lord Chancellor, Lord Simon.

Ever since the earlier brushes with Churchill the *Mirror* had been closely watched by the Government. It had annoyed them almost daily. It had criticized their mistakes; but it had also praised their triumphs. It had hit them where it hurt them most—in the minds of the public. The petrol cartoon was the final straw. They took action that was very nearly to close the *Mirror*.

On 19 March, just over a fortnight after the cartoon appeared, Cecil Thomas, the Editor, and Bartholomew were summoned by Morrison to the Home Office. He kept them waiting for a little while and when he arrived told them that the Cabinet had decided that no further warning would be given. If they overstepped the mark they would be closed down forthwith and they would remain closed down for a long time. He produced a number of the offending articles, among them the Zec cartoon, which he described as being very well drawn, 'worthy of Goebbels at his best'.

Shortly afterwards Morrison made a statement in the House of Commons announcing the action that had been taken. The row was now public property. It started off a whole series of questions in the House. Some members wanted to know who owned the paper, since a rumour had gone round that William Randolph Hearst had a large shareholding. Others said that they were fearful of action such as closure of the paper, since this amounted to the denial of freedom of speech. In Fleet Street the newspapers quickly displayed their allegiances, and only three of them showed that they agreed in part or whole with Morrison.

The debate in Parliament was pretty rugged. Tempers became heated, and the polite insults of politics were much in evidence.

Aneurin Bevan and Fred Bellenger, the Labour M.P. for Basset-
law, championed the cause of the *Mirror* with honours, Bevan
with some fine close-quarters clubbing and Bellenger with a
masterly display of rapier work.

In the House of Lords the atmosphere was equally fiery. Lord
Simon gave a stirring performance in which he came near to
out-Cassandra-ing Cassandra. He said: 'I observe that the articles
in the *Daily Mirror* which in some quarters have aroused the most
offence are signed by the nom-de-plume of Cassandra. I do not
need to remind those of your Lordships who maintain a memory
of the Greek tragedians that Cassandra came to a very sticky end.'

For Bill Connor it was a personal defeat. In his article of
Friday, 27 March 1942, which appeared simply under the name
Cassandra with no other heading, he wrote:

> This is the last wartime column you will read by Cassandra. For
> seven years, six days a week, I have written in this newspaper—
> something more than two thousand columns adding up to an astro-
> nomical number of words.
>
> Nobody has ever ghosted for me.
>
> No substitute has ever written under the mournful name of my
> Grecian nom-de-plume.
>
> I take all the blame. And if there is any credit, I take that too. This
> is the first newspaper job I have ever had. It may be the last. It all
> began with a short piece I wrote about Mrs. Rattenbury—a poor
> demented creature caught up in the coils of a tragic murder case. It
> ends today with this column—and an uneasy last laugh for Mr
> Herbert Morrison.
>
> I've had some fun. I've had some wonderful scraps. I've been right
> and I've been wrong. I've hurt people, and I've been sorry. I have
> grappled with lawyers and lunatics. I have listened to stories that
> would split your sides—and I couldn't print a line of them. I have
> listened to tales that would clutch your hearts with pity and anger—
> and, more often than not, I have been unable to lift a hand to help.
>
> That's the kind of job this is—or rather that's the kind of job this
> was.
>
> Only on two occasions has this column ceased. Once for a month
> when I was in the United States and once for a few days when I was
> reporting the war in Spain. Otherwise it's been a non-stop act. And
> all the time it has been a fight.

I remember in the early days how we used to quarrel with the advertisers—and I got worried about it. Some jumped-up pompous pickle manufacturer who was small in everything but his avarice, would write a solemn note to the editor expressing pained surprise about something I had written. Then by oblique and furtive implication he would suggest that unless his views were respected he would be reluctantly compelled to withdraw his support, i.e. his elevated advertising mission to cram his piccalilli down the throats of the credulous public. He didn't get away with it. But bigger game crashed into the scene and by 1937 the shadow of war was clear enough in this office.

By 1938 I had graduated from pickle kings to Neville Chamberlain. I fought hard against him and I fought fiercely against Munich. I had been to Germany nearly every year from 1929 to 1938 and it seemed incredible to me then, as it does now, that anybody could possibly mistake Hitler's preparations as being designed for anything but gigantic war.

I campaigned for Churchill and my support was early and violent. But since he came to power I have distrusted many of his lieutenants —and I have said so with scant respect for either their position or their feelings.

In this rough-and-tumble which has grown more bitter as the months have slipped by, I have had courageous support from my editorial colleagues of this paper that, to me at any rate, has been a remarkable thing in the records of free journalism. They have not always agreed with me—by no means—but they have let me have my say.

It has seemed to me that we have never got going in this war. We have had victories—but they have been overpowered in a terrifying succession of defeats. And the only things that have been as numerous as the defeats have been the excuses.

This war is getting old now. We are well into the third year—but in my view our efforts are disastrously below that which we will have to achieve to avoid defeat. They are further still from the zenith that alone can assure victory.

Economically, I think we are trying to temporize with a system that is discredited, outworn and totally inadequate for the emergency.

Militarily, I feel that our system has not been able to absorb and utilize the gigantic civilian army that is being amassed. The framework is rigid where it should be flexible. The administration is old fashioned where every device for efficiency is needed to see that the

military machine does not get bogged down in a morass of routine
that has nothing to do with killing Huns.

In Spain an ill-equipped army held out for three heroic years
against the Fascists backed by the arsenals of Germany and Italy. All
the odds were against them, yet they got within an ace of victory.
They were fighting for an ideal as well as their lives.

Have we the same incentive?

One answer—and it is only a partial answer—has come from
Singapore.

In the House of Commons you will have heard how criticism is
received. The Government is extraordinarily sensitive.

They are far too glib with the shameful rejoinder that those who
do not agree with them are subversive—and even traitors.

Yet the whole course of their conduct from Dunkirk to the inclu-
sion of Sir Stafford Cripps in the War Cabinet has showed that they
have followed the advice of their critics. Yesterday's proceedings
prove how determined they are henceforth to do without this advice.

But that is now all over. You will have heard the storm and read
the debate about the *Daily Mirror*.

I cannot and will not change my policy. In the past I have ap-
plauded politicians who have got out rather than knuckle under.
Today I applaud my own funeral. I believe, like Edmund Burke,
that the Government should understand that it holds good in this
country that 'He that wrestles with us strengthens our nerves and
sharpens our skill. Our antagonist is our helper!'

And I also believe, like Burke, that 'the people will never give up
their liberties but under some delusion'.

Churchill told a former colleague of his that 'there are paths of
service open in wartime which are not open in the days of peace, and
some of these paths may be paths to honour'.

I, who have not transgressed, am shortly following the Prime
Minister's advice. I am still a comparatively young man and I propose
to see whether the rifle is a better weapon than the printed word.

Mr Morrison can have my pen—but not my conscience.

Mr Morrison can have my silence—but not my self-respect.'

One doubts that Bill Connor ever wrote a more majestic and
dignified column. It was certainly a more powerful article than
his obituary of Churchill written many years later, which many
people regard as the finest piece he ever wrote.

Mr Herbert Morrison's comments are not recorded.

Within the month Bill Connor had joined the Army and had been sent to an O.C.T.U. camp at Llandrindod Wells in Wales. He did not enjoy it much, partly because of the weather—it can be very wet in Radnor—and partly because the military, and in particular those members of it who had been offended by his gibes, had at last got their hands on him. In particular there was one training officer at the camp who disliked him intensely and made his dislike known by being very difficult all the time. However, he made a mistake in thinking that a man who is handy with the pen cannot be handy with anything else. Connor and some of his fellow trainee officers were in the local pub, the Llanarch Arms, one evening, when in walked the training officer. They studiously ignored him, to his obvious irritation. He asked them—singling Connor out as spokesman for the group—why they did not stand in the presence of an officer. Connor replied that it was because they were not on duty. The officer, still trying to force his point, then asked why they did not stand in the presence of a gentleman. He did not see the giant trap being prepared for him. Connor asked him if he was talking to them in the guise of an officer or of a gentleman. The man replied that he was now speaking to him as a gentleman.

'In that case, as you claim to be a gentleman', said Connor, 'perhaps you'd care to step outside a moment.'

The training officer did so—and received a bloody nose for his insults. Connor was put back a month on the course. But the victory was his.

When he finally passed out from the O.C.T.U. camp, Connor was posted to an anti-aircraft battery at Deal. But even this was not without its difficulties. He had originally asked to join the Royal Tank Regiment but his application was turned down and instead he joined the Royal Artillery. Here he had to learn the mystique of gunnery. Never the greatest mathematician, right from the time he was at school, the world of trigonometry as applied to making great lumps of steel, propelled by high explosives, land on or about their target, totally appalled and bemused him. Sines, cosines and tangents were something he believed must have been thought up by a particularly twisted creature hidden somewhere in the depths of the War Office as a special revenge for all the needling articles he had written about the stupidity and inefficiency of the military mind. The whole subject was far beyond him. When the time came for the final written exam, he was almost frantic. Kindly comrades —including an ex-schoolmaster who was used to dealing with obtuse pupils—spent hours giving him private tuition. Finally he resolved that the only solution to this problem was to cheat in the examination. But how? Small crib sheets were always spotted, and it is pretty hard to read notes written on the cuff of a khaki serge shirt. Then he had a brilliant idea. On the theory that it is best to hide a stolen tree in a wood, he began to construct his master crib sheet. In the class rooms that had been taken over for the training of gunnery officers there were a number of very big wooden tables, the sort that are about ten feet long by three feet wide, and are usually covered in pencil and ink writing with an artless penknife engraving here and there. Connor carefully selected the one at which he usually sat and began to write out on it, in huge child-like letters, all that he would need to know for the exam. He added—still in the same forged childish hand— diagrams and sketches. When it was completed it was the finest and most complete treatise on ballistics imaginable. And totally indistinguishable from any of the other desks to the unsuspicious eye. He was now fully prepared for the exam.

On the day it was held, he and his other fellow officers went, as usual, to the classroom. To his utter horror, on arriving at his desk, he found that the great oaken cheat sheet was gone. His table had been replaced by another. Frantically, he and a friend scoured the place, and found the right table in another room. They grabbed it, rushed back to the classroom, and made the switch just in time. He passed the exam.

But if the theoretical side of gunnery had been carefully side-stepped, the practical side posed its own problems. Connor was not a very good gunner. On one occasion, during some practice firing, he nearly managed to shoot down Deal Gasworks. It was very fortunate for the inhabitants of Deal, let alone any Luftwaffe pilot, that Connor was soon afterwards given an overseas posting.

In the late summer of 1943 he found himself on board a troop-carrying ship bound for North Africa. His movements were uncertain. There was a possibility that he might join the Eighth Army. On the other hand there was also a sporting chance that he would be sent to Burma to join Frank Owen who had started a paper for the troops called *SEAC News*. In the final event, he did neither.

Hugh Cudlipp, who was a colonel with the newly formed British Army Newspaper Unit, was in Naples. He heard that Bill Connor was in the Mediterranean area and managed to get him posted to B.A.N.U. In late September Connor joined him.

This is a convenient moment to look a little more closely at Cudlipp. He was born in 1913 in Cardiff, the son of a commercial traveller. From 1927 to 1932 he worked on a number of provincial newspapers in Cardiff and Manchester. He then came to Fleet Street and joined the *Sunday Chronicle* as features editor. And it was from here that he joined the *Daily Mirror* on the same day as Bill Connor in 1935.

Physically Hugh Cudlipp is compactly built, though he is deceptive for he looks stockier than, in fact, he is. He stands like a boxer, head forward and slightly down, tucked into his shoulders. The lower jaw juts forward pugnaciously, as though daring you to take a swipe at it. When he speaks, the words appear to be ground out through the partially-clenched teeth. The consonants slap you in the face. His hands (or are they fists?) holding the ever-present cigar are stabbed into the air to make the spoken point even more forceful, as though he were stubbing out the cigar on one of many aerial, invisible ashtrays hovering about him.

He is, by nature, a pugnacious man. You take him on 'at your peril', to use the title of one of his books. He is also a superb editorial journalist. The title 'The Great Sub-Editor', bestowed on him by others in Fleet street, is not lightly earned. Nor is it in any way the least derogatory. His own writing reflects the character of the man. It is short, crisp, punchy—and violent. Where two words would do, Cudlipp uses three. Only they are shorter and usually have an Anglo-Saxon origin and sentiment. If Connor, as a writer, can be said to have used words like a cudgel, then Cudlipp uses them like a knuckleduster. He likes to get in close. When, in 1960, the *Mirror* published a front page that simply read 'Mr. K. (if you will pardon an olde English phrase) DON'T BE SO BLOODY RUDE! P.S. Who do you think you are? Stalin?', the influence—if not the hand itself— of Hugh Cudlipp was plainly discernible to students of rugged writing. That is the way the man writes. Bluntly. Simply. Directly. With no frills, no camouflage. And, as often as not, it makes BLOODY GOOD SENSE.

And it was his large-bull-in-a-very-small-china-shop approach that got him the man he wanted to join his newspaper unit, Bill Connor.

The purpose of the British Army Newspaper Unit was, not surprisingly, to produce a newspaper for the British troops in Italy. But it posed its own problems. The Germans were being fast driven back past the ankle and up the boot of Italy. Finding time—and the facilities—to produce a newspaper was a very big problem. But it was managed, and managed well. *Union Jack* (or 'Onion Duke' as it was known by its devotees) appeared regularly and was enjoyed by all. Somehow it managed to keep some of its own colour, even after the emasculating efforts of the official censors. It was not entirely filled with Army propaganda.

One of the reasons for its success was that it was, in spirit if not in fact, a miniature *Daily Mirror* in khaki. Cudlipp was the Commanding Officer. In his officers' mess and on his editorial staff he had Bill Connor and Peter Wilson from the *Mirror*. They were a very unholy trinity. To add a necessary air of respect-ability and tone there was Hammond Innes, who had come by way of Brendan Bracken's *Financial News* and an ack-ack battery in Sicily. Later on, Bill Herbert, another chum from the *Mirror*, was to join them, via the R.A.F. Others from Fleet Street included the cartoonist Jon, creator of the Two Types, Ralph Thackeray, now of the *Sunday Telegraph*, and at one time after the war, of *Public Opinion*, and Cyril James of the *People*. They—and a few more besides—managed to bring out *Union Jack* in Naples, Bari, Rome, Florence, Bologna, Venice and elsewhere before the war finally ended.

Their Mess was fairly typical, except that it may well have been a trifle rougher than most. Certainly, with two men as boisterous as Connor and Cudlipp, it should have been. There were the usual

Fc

schoolboy jokes. One of the favourite ones involved dressing up a full-size articulated artist's model in battle dress complete with general's tabs on the lapels, and sitting it on the lavatory bowl. The door would then be left slightly ajar, so that any unsuspecting visitor who entered would see the dimly-lit figure and immediately crash to attention and stumble back with a flustered: 'Awfully sorry . . . Sir!'

To help pass the time, Connor and Peter Wilson evolved a game that was, at the same time, constructive and destructive. It was called Dictionary Cricket. It was a very simple game. One or other of them would specify a page number in the dictionary. He would then call out, say, 'Third word from the bottom, left-hand column'. If his opponent knew the correct definition of the word selected in this fashion the questioner—or 'bowler'—would have to buy the 'batsman' a drink. If he did not, then the batsman was out and had to buy the bowler a drink. It was constructive in that they both became extraordinarily expert at word-definitions. It was destructive in that there were—as one might guess—eleven batsman in each side, and therefore twenty-two drinks per game. The drink they chose was invariably a moderately ruinous mixture of fresh lemon juice and Italian brandy.

It was a fairly relaxed Mess with few rules. But there was one to which they kept rigidly. And that was that all officers had to be correctly dressed for breakfast. On one occasion—after a very heavy Dictionary Cricket match the night before—Peter Wilson came down to breakfast, nursing a giant hangover and still in his dressing-gown. He was immediately sent back to dress. As he was painfully digging out a shirt, he was astounded to see a small bird fly out of it. At first he did not believe his eyes and he called Connor in to verify that the bird did in fact exist. Connor was able to do this, but the two of them were viewed with grave suspicion when they reported the incident to the others.

The main problem for all of them was that of acute boredom. They had more than enough time on their hands, and the work they had to do to produce the newspaper only took up a small part of it. When they did have the opportunity to write, they all took great pains over it, polishing and repolishing the words until they were as perfect as they felt they could ever be. Some of their spare time was taken up with sight-seeing, though this obviously presented its own problems. However, Connor did manage to see a great deal of Italy during the three years he spent there. He even managed to ride a motorcycle up Mount Vesuvius while it was erupting. Some of the time was taken up with eating and drinking, reading copiously and arguing furiously. It was a very happy Mess, despite the almost total lack of stimulus and opportunity to write in the way to which they were used.

Hugh Cudlipp recalls one incident which, although humorous, nearly split the Mess in two. It certainly divided them into cat-lovers and cat-haters.

They were at the time billeted in a sprawling apartment of fast-fading elegance in Naples.

Sharing the apartment with them was a lively, shiny, black cat called Catrina, of whom Bill Connor was inordinately fond. She was an extrovert who spent the whole evening performing the most astonishing tricks, scrambling up curtains, leaping distances of ten feet, rushing round the room until she collapsed in fits of giddiness. Catrina was a lovable animal; but there were those who considered cats—especially Italian street moggies—unhygienic.

Dissent was rife. Anti-Catrina mutterings could be heard plainly. The only sensible thing to do was to hold a proper trial.

Catrina had—as her prosecuting counsel—Peter Wilson, a strong anti-cat man. But for her defence she had Bill Connor.

'Think, gentlemen,' said Connor. 'Humanity is locked in an ugly embrace which dwarfs the First World War to the significance of a minor military exercise on Salisbury Plain. At this very moment thousands of heavy bombers are pulverizing the Germans, civilian and military alike, on mighty sorties from British airfields. In the Far East the vast forces of the United States and Britain are moving towards the final crunch with the Japanese. The Russians are conducting the greatest scorched earth policy in the history of war, fighting like madmen for every inch of their homeland. And all you have to argue about is two penn'orth of catshit neatly deposited in the Neapolitan bidet of a revolting Italian Fascist who has escaped to the hills until all is safe for his return.'

Connor's advocacy won the day. Catrina would be allowed to live, only she would henceforth be known as Latrina. This last was Hugh Cudlipp's ruling for it was he, as senior officer, who had presided over the trial.

However, Catrina's reprieve was short-lived. A few days later she crawled into the apartment leaving a trail of blood behind her. She had been stoned by some children in the street and had come home to die.

The war dragged on. The big events in Connor's life, as with his fellow officers, were the small events. Like the time he and a couple of friends went for a meal in a café, parking their jeep outside where they could see it, just the other side of a low wall. When they came out they found that some light-fingered Italians had removed all the wheels and left it perched on four neat piles of bricks. Or the time that Bill Connor found that another less-than-trustworthy manservant had been helping himself to a bottle of his Italian brandy. Connor fixed him quite simply by topping up the bottle with lighter fuel. Within a few short weeks Agostino was unwittingly drinking the finest château-bottled Ronsonol. But despite even these amusing incidents, life was one of unmitigated boredom. And boredom was the one thing above all else with which Bill Connor was unable to cope.

Hugh Cudlipp described him once as the 'reluctant soldier'. He was undoubtedly that. All that this period proved to Connor was that war is loathsome, and that the pen—in addition to being mightier than the sword—is considerably more interesting.

CHAPTER SIX
'AS I WAS SAYING...'

BILL CONNOR's war did not end until 1946. It was not until August of that year that he was finally demobbed. Three months after V.E. Day—when everyone had hoped the war was over and they would soon be home—he had been posted to Venice, still with the British Army Newspaper Unit, to await his turn for demobilization. It did not come as quickly as he hoped; indeed it was deferred for nine months. This delay was certainly the most arduous period of the whole war for him. All his *Daily Mirror* friends had returned home and were gradually readjusting themselves to civilian life after so many years away. Connor fretted for a year, bored to desperation, concerned about his family at home. His parents, who were in their seventies by now, were having a difficult time and his wife was worried because their first son, who had been born in 1942, had developed asthma. Added to this was the fact that the food situation was bad in England and the weather vile. It was a very cold winter and fuel was desperately hard to get. After six years of war, the country was finding it very difficult to come to terms with peace. The Labour Government, elected with an overwhelming majority in 1945, was discovering that it is a mighty hard task to patch up the effects of war. Rationing and shortages were the order of the day.

In one way, however, Bill Connor could have been counted a little more fortunate than many, for he was in a warm climate and an occupying army is never really short of food and clothing. Physically he was well, but the mental strain was hard to bear. His letters home during this wasted year show very clearly his attitude. They lack the spark of earlier ones, and are full of references to his longing to be back. Earlier he had spoken warmly of the Italian countryside and the people he had come to love; the letters from Venice are brave little ones which tried—and failed— to reassure his family and friends at home.

While he had been away great changes had been taking place

at the *Mirror*. To start with, Bartholomew had become Chairman in place of John Cowley, late in 1944. The brave spirit of the paper, which had been its hallmark during the black days of 1940-42, had become a little threadbare round the edges. Like the soldiers returning home, the *Mirror* appeared to be stunned by peace. Nothing seemed quite real. It had a brief—and glorious—return to its old style with the 1945 election and its support of the Labour Party. But after that—journalistic anaemia. Newsprint was rationed, so the paper had to be thin. But even if it had had unlimited paper, the *Mirror* would have remained emaciated for some time. It had been run for four or five years on a skeleton staff. In Bartholomew, it had a very strong head—but with no body to support it. A number of members of the pre-war board were, by 1945, either dead or retired. Like a weak and defeated country, the *Mirror* was ready for a new dynasty.

Philip Zec, whose V.E. Day cartoon showing a wounded British soldier proffering a garland which read, 'Victory and Peace in Europe' and saying 'Here you are! Don't lose it again!', was every bit as brilliant as the petrol cartoon that had got the paper into trouble, had been invited to join the board of the *Sunday Pictorial* to run the art and pictures side of both papers. When he started the job, he found an appalling state of affairs. The syndication department needed a great deal of work—and a number of violent rows—to get it going again. As Bill Herbert, who by this time had got back to the *Mirror*, put in a letter to Connor, the *Mirror* was 'very dull, and its management inept . . . it would help if they made up their minds whether they want the *Mirror* to be a newspaper or a daily magazine'. This last remark was a further reflection on the fact that newsprint was rationed, and that the Mirror had chosen to eke out its meagre helping by filling the paper with magazine-style articles and editorials. The news was notable for its almost total absence. The *Mirror* was talking about the brave new world that was to come, in the hope that it would take its readers' minds off the rough, raw one in which they were living.

Hugh Cudlipp had returned from Italy and had taken up his job as editor of the *Sunday Pictorial* once more. He was to remain there for only three years until a disagreement with Bartholomew led to his going to the *Daily Express* for a two-year sabbatical. Cecil Thomas, the editor of the *Daily Mirror* since 1934 and Bartholomew's chief lieutenant, was only a couple of years away from handing the editorship over to Sylvester Bolam. Some members of the pre-war staff had been killed; others had drifted away on their return home.

The war effort had taken its toll. The *Mirror* was punch-drunk; its management were unsteady and desperately groping to find their way back to the dynamism of the pre-war years. And Bill Connor, kicking his heels in Venice, was bored and frustrated.

When, however, he finally arrived back in England in the late autumn of 1946, he was a changed man. The moment he had something worth while to do and could get back to the job he loved, he threw himself into it with renewed vigour. If the years spent writing for B.A.N.U. had had any beneficial effect, it was to make his writing even more pungent, more barbed, more polished, more witty. He was like a man unfettered; and it showed very much in his column.

His first post-war column—and one that is well-remembered —appeared on the morning of Monday, 23 September 1946. It started with the words:

'As I was saying before I was interrupted, it is a powerful hard thing to please all the people all the time . . .'

Within a matter of months he had been sent on a round-the-world trip by the paper to take a look at what had been going on in his absence. He went to Palestine a few short months before it became Israel. He saw for himself the beginning of the birth of that brave new nation. From there he went to Karachi and observed the partition of Pakistan from India. He moved on to Singapore. And to Malaya, which was slowly boiling up to the terrorist activities that were to engulf it a year later. And he went finally to Australia, which he loved. The country fascinated him and one suspects that had he been a little younger he may well have been tempted to emigrate there. Certainly it was the country he advised people who wanted to emigrate to choose.

He had left on this journey only a few weeks after the birth of his second child, a daughter who was named Mary. Shortly after his return he was involved in another family affair, this time of a tragic nature.

His parents had come to live, towards the end of the war, in a small cottage opposite the one in which he lived at Skirmett. His father had immediately re-immersed himself in all the old activities of his retirement. They had been interrupted by the war when he had volunteered to go back into the Civil Service and had been posted for a while to Bath. But now he was able to get back to them. He nursed his allotment with loving care, and protected his broad beans with great vigour from the rampages of his grandson and sundry other small boys. And once again he was a choirmaster, this time at the beautiful church in Hambleden village. It was a couple of miles away, but he enjoyed the walk to and from choir practice. On 27 January 1948, the following article appeared under the familiar 'spectacles' motif in the *Daily Mirror*:

Exactly twelve days ago, at 6.10 p.m., an elderly gentleman put on his fawn-coloured raincoat, his grey cap and set out to go to the local choir practice two and a half miles away.

He had done the journey many times before, was cheerful and in good health. At five minutes to seven he was noticed within a hundred yards of the church.

From that moment when he was seen standing at a crossroads, he has not been sighted again.

Here in this year 1948, with its enormous mechanism of identity cards, passports, flying-squad patrols and all the rest of the careful documentation of human activities, a kindly old chap just disappears. He had six pounds on him, and a gold watch engraved with his initials W.H.C. He was happy, liked walking and had no worries.

There are near-by woods into which he might well have strayed but they have been repeatedly searched by the police, by R.A.F. squads and by as knowledgeable a crowd of farmers, gamekeepers, beaters and poachers as ever set an appreciative eye on a cock-pheasant.

There is a river a mile and a half further on but it has yielded nothing. Bus-drivers, postmen, tradesmen, roadmen and lock-keepers have all been questioned. They have also seen nothing.

Out-buildings, sheds and hayricks for miles around have been examined.

No result. No trace. No clue.

That man was my father.

Here in a newspaper office we deal in this sort of thing. It makes news. To me it is part of my trade—provided it comes normally and impersonally over the ticker-tape, the telephone or by mail. You can look at it critically, weigh up its value and assess its interest—always provided it is someone else.

But when it comes crashing in on the quietude of your own home, it makes you feel more than strange—even plaintive. And you think: 'Out of all the teeming millions of this overcrowded isle, why pick on me?'

And when the national and evening papers get you on the telephone (not knowing you are in the trade) and ask you with tact, good sense and even sympathy (Royal Press Commission, please note) you feel slightly disembodied as you go over the familiar, mournful description again:

'Name, William Henry Connor. Age 75. Last seen at Hambleden, Bucks, 6.55 p.m. January 14. Fawn raincoat. Grey cloth cap. Walking stick. Brown shoes. Clean shaven. Height 5ft 10ins. May be suffering from loss of memory.'

You might think that contented old gentlemen just don't disappear these days.

You might think that the network of modern registration has too fine a mesh to lose ordinary law-abiding citizens going quietly about their business.

You might think that efficient friendly police and good neighbours prepared to give days of their time in combing the undergrowth and ranging the fields, would have some luck attendant on their efforts.

But you would be wrong. For they haven't.

Not yet . . .'

A month after he wrote this article, Bill Connor's father was found. He had fallen into the river and was drowned. There was no clue as to how he had got into the river. An open verdict was returned.

The death of Henry Connor had a further tragic consequence. His wife, who had been quite free from her bouts of depression, became ill yet again. This time it was far more serious than either of the two previous occasions and she soon had to be moved back into hospital, first at Taplow in Berkshire and then to a hospital near Northampton. She never recovered sufficiently to leave. She died shortly before Christmas, 1954.

The late 1940s and the early years of the fifties were a very black period for Bill Connor. In addition to the death of his father—and later of his mother—things were not going well for him at the *Daily Mirror*. The paper had seemed to recover from its immediate post-war malaise only to have a relapse. Harry Guy Bartholomew reached his 65th birthday in 1949, but showed no sign of retiring. Indeed, his wheeling and dealing had become a little more frenzied than was normal. He was drinking heavily and doubtless his judgement was being impaired as a result. In addition, 1948 had brought a new editor to the paper, Sylvester Bolam, who had replaced Cecil Thomas. Bolam had, in a front page article on his appointment as editor, written of the *Mirror*:

> The *Mirror* is a sensational newspaper. . . . We believe in the sensational presentation of news and views, especially important news and views, as a necessary and valuable public service in these days of mass readership and democratic responsibility. We shall go on being sensational to the best of our ability. . . . We shall make our mistakes but at least we are alive.

These were brave words, especially in the light of the paper's internal situation. And, sadly, they were somewhat prophetic. In 1949 the *Mirror* did make a mistake, one which was to effect Bolam personally. The *Mirror* was indicted for contempt of court over the Haigh murder case. It was found guilty and Bolam, as editor, was held responsible. He spent three months in Brixton Prison; the paper was fined £10,000.

In addition to these troubles there were others. Many people were unhappy with Bolam as editor. Bill Connor was one of them. He did not like Bolam personally. Normally this would not have mattered much, but with all his other personal problems, life became very difficult. And he became very restless. His column had been changed around, its appearance altered. He began to think that his position at the *Mirror* was not quite as stable as it had been, that they might even be thinking of getting rid of him. The offers that he received almost continuously from other newspapers suddenly took on a new tempting look. He wondered whether he should consider them a little more seriously than he had done in the past. The wooing from the Beaverbrook Press was particularly strong. He decided to talk it over with Cecil King, who after the palace revolution that deposed Bartholomew in 1951, was soon to become Chairman. King persuaded him to stay and offered him the editorship of a small and ailing magazine called *Public Opinion*. Connor accepted it. It seemed to him that here was a way to keep a little distance between himself and Bolam and to stay with the *Mirror* for which he had a great affection and loyalty. So in January 1950 he took on the new responsibility, while still writing a regular Cassandra column for the *Mirror*.

It was not really a success. In fact, the eighteen months during which he ran it proved to Connor that, while he may have been a writer of some merit, he was certainly no editor. But it was doomed from the start. King had wanted a serious magazine within the *Mirror* group of publications. Bartholomew had not. King had thought that *Public Opinion*—which had been founded in 1861 as a 'radical review'—could in time and with careful nursing become a serious competitor to the *New Statesman* or the *Spectator*. Bart was just not interested in it; it was not popular journalism. And since Bart controlled the purse-strings, the necessary money to make it a success was not forthcoming.

Despite this and the fact that he was not first-class editor material, Connor enjoyed himself. He managed to persuade all kinds of people to write for the magazine. Grahame Hutton, Alan Fairclough, Douglas Houghton, Virginia Vernon, Stephen Spender, Arthur C. Clarke, Alex Comfort, Stephen Swingler, Dingle Foot, Patrick Sergeant, William Sansom, Woodrow Wyatt, Konni Zilliacus, Kenneth Adam, Francis Williams, Mervyn Stockwood, A. J. P. Taylor, were among the contributors and regular writers. The magazine usually ran to 28 pages of well-balanced articles and editorials, critiques and crosswords and the usual personal column advertisements offering manuscript typing, yoga lessons and a sure way of giving up smoking. In his early days as editor, Connor took great delight in writing not only the editorial articles, but also the correspondence that they were supposed to have provoked. One week he would adopt the guise of 'Disgusted, Cheltenham' and fulminate in true militant style; the next, he would take on the silken tones of the university don and write spuriously erudite letters on some unbelievably obscure subject. Later, of course, when the magazine had gained a little strength of its own, the letters used were genuine. But in these early days quite a few of his friends and family were surprised to find their names appended to letters that they had not sent to *Public Opinion*.

One letter in particular—and also one of the genuine ones— was from George Bernard Shaw, written six months before his death in 1950. It was one that Connor particularly prized.

> My first appearance in print was in a boy's paper: two lines in the correspondence column. But it was in *Public Opinion* that I made my debut as a critic and controversialist. The only result was an emergency meeting of my uncles to discuss the horrifying news that the Shaw family had produced an Atheist. I still hold that thinkers who are not militant atheists in their teens will have no religion at all when they are 40. I was already a Creative Evolutionist in the bud. I have ever since had a warm corner in my heart for *Public Opinion*.

The issue of Friday, 22 June 1951, bore a short paragraph under the magazine's masthead saying: 'We regret to announce that as from this issue, the publication of *Public Opinion* will be suspended.' Rather inappropriately it carried an advertisement on the last page but one with a headline that read 'SECRETS OF SUCCESSFUL WRITING. Learn how to make money by writing for the Press.'

Despite his unease and unhappiness during this period Bill Connor was turning out some very good Cassandra columns. His pre-war writing had been sombre and sharp, occasionally with a twist-of-lemon-smile at the end. But some time during or even after the war he had learnt to write in a much more openly humorous manner. And strangely—almost as though he were trying to use them as an antidote to his unrest—some of the funniest colums were written during this period. When they were about food, they were masterly. This one appeared in June 1949:

How I like My Cabbage

O listen to the words: 'BOILED CABBAGE.' Remove the coarse outer leaves of the cabbage and cut off the stalk. Either halve or quarter the cabbage and wash thoroughly in cold water. Drain thoroughly and put in a large saucepan with a plentiful amount of boiling salted water. When the water is again on the boil, allow from ten to fifteen minutes fast boiling according to size and freshness of the cabbage. Cabbages boiled for longer than this are apt to be flabby and flavourless.

FLABBY AND FLAVOURLESS!

The words are cripples—cripples bleeding to death. Letters hooked and handcuffed together—hamstrung and powerless. FLABBY AND FLAVOURLESS INDEED! The phrase is a crawling compliment.

Boiled cabbage à l'Anglaise is something compared with which steamed coarse newsprint bought from bankrupt Finnish salvage dealers and heated over smoky oil stoves is an exquisite delicacy.

Boiled British cabbage is something lower than ex-army blankets stolen by dispossessed Goanese dosshouse-keepers who used them to cover busted down henhouses in the slum district of Karachi, found them useless, threw them in anger into the Indus, where they were recovered by convicted beachcombers with grappling irons, who cut them in strips with shears and stewed them in sheepdip before they were sold to dying beggars.

Boiled Cabbage!

Yet if you will come into the garden this very night, but not earlier than ten minutes past eleven, when the sun is yards deep below the rim of the world and the pale North-West has shut its eyes, you will hear something to your advantage if you listen.

It is English cabbage a-growing.

The sound of Harbinger and Jersey Wakefield and Velocity (millionaires' yachts were never named as well as these) and Roundhead and Primo and Cotswold Queen and Daniel's Defiance and Enfield and Beefheart (what a title) and Myatt's Early Offenham all rustling in the cool and gentle summer night.

Listen! Hear them! A rubbery rustling noise. The force of delectable greenness on the march.

The muscular sigh of strong leaves growing stronger. The s-t-r-e-t-c-h of white hearts bursting out from verdant folds.

Cool night rain may fall long before the June larks set up their intolerable twitter of compulsive happiness and into the cool crevices of Beefheart (and his consort, Cotswold Queen), the diamond splash of cold clear water will run in rivulets and gather in bright globules ready for the morning sun. Here is freshness—springy, moist and crisp.

Here is the young and eager garden life before it is murdered and done to unspeakable death—the corpse of which is called Boiled Cabbage.

There are thirty-one ways of cooking a cabbage. Not boiling it—but cooking it.

May I play you a little culinary music? Just one excerpt? 'Quarter the cabbage, shred very finely and chop.' Now sit down. Rest awhile and switch off that darned wireless. Drop that horrible game of cards and come over here.

'Put the pieces into a thick saucepan—thick, thick, thick—and plop in four ounces of butter' (butter from non-psychotic cows, blast you), 'and simmer gently for thirty-four minutes.'

'Stir constantly. Do not brown!'

What do you think this is—a gas chamber? 'When tender and of light golden colour' (the colour of corn five days after it has been cut from the side of dark-earthed slopes facing south, south-east) 'add one ounce of chopped onion and a little chopped parsley' (planted by a lean but lovely virgin with green fingers) 'and simmer for nine minutes.

'Remove from the fire' (smokeless embers glowing a dull red of course and may Allah trample upon all gasometers), 'and when nearly cold add one tablespoonful of white breadcrumbs, two well beaten eggs' (blend down, you Buff Orpington Beauties), 'and season with salt and pepper. Put a clean cloth in a basin. Place the large outer cabbage leaves in it. Fill with cabbage mixture. Tie up. Boil for one hour in boiling salted water.'

Have a glass of cool dark beer and let the blighters get on with their wretched cards.

'Remove the cloth. Place the cabbage on a hot dish and serve with hot melted butter whilst reciting "The Scholar Gypsy" with compliments to Matthew Arnold.'

And don't forget the thick red rashers of Tewkesbury peach-fed ham and the infant potatoes ruthlessly murdered in their little cradle-graves long before they were golf ball size.

See what I mean?

If boiled cabbage is not to your liking then try this:

M'SELLE ANISETTE

One day last week in a London police court a man who looked as if he'd been practising swallow dives off the top board into a swimming bath three days after they'd pulled the plug out, was charged with being drunk. After he had pleaded guilty, the magistrate put the routine question to him: 'Have you anything you wish to say to me?' 'Yes,' he replied simply, 'it was Anisette.' 'She's nothing to do with the case,' replied the Beak testily, 'Pay ten shillings.'

Pity.

Anisette is not a girl. She's a drink. The kind of drink you should know about. May I explain?

You can't appreciate the stuff in London—where it's pretty hard to get. Nor in Marseilles or Bandol or Ajaccio or Athens—where it is easy to get. You've got to drink Anisette in a shaded bar in Tunis run by a great crafty hulk of a man called Max. He lives in a side street off the Avenue Jules-Ferry. The temperature is 110 in the shade. The Arabs are screaming like parakeets. A shoeshine boy from the Casbah has just spat neatly on your shoes—Arab salesmanship to get the contract.

And you don't feel so good.

The shadow of last night hangs on you like an electrically heated horsehair blanket, coated with hot glue. It is mid-day. You are not very clever at steering yourself towards Max's. You feel as if you are wearing a cylindrical glass overcoat on top of the blanket. It is hard to get through doorways because it is so wide. And who wants to stand ankle-deep in broken glass?

Max doesn't move when you go in. But he winks. And you hear the great leathery eyelid rattle over the crafty eyeball like a Venetian blind; then it lifts again lopsidedly as if one cord is broken. Nothing is said.

Max takes a bottle from the shelf and pours a clear fluid from it into a tall glass. You add water to it. Max shovels in splintered ice. Meet M'selle Anisette.

Drink it. It tastes rather like the distillate you'd get from good quality toothpaste and liquorice. Rather clinical. Anisette has the enormous advantage of making you think you're doing yourself good.

It leaps down your burning windpipe like a freezing mountain stream into the battered punch-bag of your guts.

Message from Guts to Brain: 'WHAT THE HELL'S GOING ON UP THERE?'

Brain to Guts: 'HOLD EVERYTHING, BUD—WE MEAN JUST THAT.'

More Anisette. Try drinking it between clenched teeth. The ice packs up against your molars like driftwood against a weir. Good. The cylindrical glass overcoat disintegrates. The gluey blanket disappears and Max looks only half leprous. More please. The idiot sunshine that has been booting the back off your eyeballs stops and starts to whistle.

I said whistle.

In Tunis you can *hear* the sunshine if you listen carefully especially with M'selle Anisette. It's up in the high-pitched class marked 'Dogs Only'.

Encore, s'il vous plaît. The brain begins to sparkle and glitter in the dark cave of your skull. Guts glow. And Max does his stuff again. Good fellow.

High up above the hot stink of French North Africa in the snowy Atlas crags among the alpine flowers of pure delight is where Anisette was born.

What a girl!

In January 1950 Bill and Mair Connor's third child was born —a second son, named Frank after Connor's favourite uncle. In the late summer of that year they moved house. They went from the small rented house in Skirmett to an old rectory in the village of Fingest, less than a mile away. Connor could not bear to be separated from his beloved Hambleden Valley. The new house was bigger and very much more characterful. It was a part-Georgian and part 16th-century flint cottage. Connor adored it— and it provided him with a little private joke. His previous house had been called the Old Forge. He had been very amused to receive letters from his bank addressed to him—with a typing error—as 'W. N. Connor, The Old Forger . . .'. The new house, being an old rectory, led to a spate of letters and circulars being sent to him as 'Rev. W. N. Connor'. He delighted in his transmogrification from crook to cleric.

The move to the new house reinforced Bill Connor's love for the Chilterns and the people of the area. Throughout his life he had the knack of splitting his working life from his family life. He developed it to the point that if a member of his family circle were to meet him for lunch during the week when he was working, they would find a subtle, but nonetheless distinct, change in his personality. The protective shell that he wore in his capacity as a journalist was obviously put on with the business suit in the morning and taken off in the evening. He would be familiar—and yet in certain ways a little distant.

This dual personality led quite naturally to Connor having two distinct sets of friends. There were the dozen or so *Mirror* colleagues and business friends that he had in London, and an equal number of local people in the country. It was rare that the newspaper friends came down to the country for week-ends, and rarer still that the country friends met him in London.

Two of Bill Connor's closest country friends were George Harman, a builder who lived in Fingest, and Len Wise, who lived in a nearby village and had been in the Home Guard with Connor in the early days of the war. Wise had at one time been a 'gentleman's gentleman' to a certain peer, who had the eccentric habit of ringing up his employee very late and very drunk from one of the many night-clubs he patronized, saying 'Wise, tell me where I am, and then come and fetch me.' Harman's family have lived in the area for years and he knows as much about Buckinghamshire folk-lore as any man. Connor was always fascinated by this aspect of country life. He loved to hear old superstitions and pieces of folk-lore. He collected them—and on quite a number of occasions wrote about them. In their company he was able to relax completely. They in turn provided him with a friendship that was not based on a false admiration for Cassandra, the famous journalist, but a liking for Bill Connor, the man who lived in the same village and drank in the same pubs as them. They originally met in pubs and it was in pubs that the friendship flowered. Indeed, it was the common denominator of good beer and friendly banter that led them on a number of regular and sometimes hilarious escapades. One such was the annual Parsley Seed Hunt. Every year, Connor, Wise, Harman and a few other local friends would go on a day's outing 'to buy parsley seed'. The event always took place on the day of Thame Show, which was only about twelve miles away. The strategy was very simple. They would all drive to Thame, call in at a seed merchant to buy a 3d packet of parsley seed, and pop into the pub next door.

Gc

Since, at that time, the pubs were open all day for the show, and Thame has a good dozen or so, they were able to go on a very long and enjoyable pub crawl and be able to return with the perilously thin, but nevertheless true, excuse that they were sorry they were late but they had been buying parsley seed, and would then be able to produce a small packet as proof.

Another similar excuse for a trip round the best pubs was the annual Brewster Sessions when Connor, who had a car, would take his landlord friend from pre-war days, Freddie Cutler, to Marlow to renew his publican's licence. Since the Sessions lasted most of the day and they often had to wait their turn, they usually had a very enjoyable time.

1951, as well as marking Bill Connor's failure as a magazine editor, was a turning point in his career as a writer. With the closure of *Public Opinion*, Connor was brought back into the *Mirror* with a little more prominence. He certainly felt happier about it. He was enjoying his writing again after the worries and problems of an uncomfortable editorial chair. But, most importantly, he began to travel.

Every journalist worth his salt knows the value of travelling around the world. It presents him with new influences, new challenges, new viewpoints, new perspectives. A story seen from an office in London takes on a wholly new look when seen at first hand. Bill Connor had of course travelled a good deal before the war. He had also travelled a little since the end of the war. He had been to Germany to see how it was beginning to recover. He had been on his first round-the-world trip, but this was made up of a series of specific events. In all these instances he was acting as a reporter and not as a commentator. He had no time to get the smell of the places he visited, to identify the undercurrents and get to know the people.

He had also travelled to various places in Europe that year in connection with *Public Opinion*. But in December, he set out on what was really the first of his trips abroad as a commentator. He had no specific brief other than that he was going out to have a look at one or two things that he was interested in as a newspaperman. He wanted particularly to see the Middle and Far East.

He flew to Beirut, then on to Karachi, Hong Kong and

Singapore. He spent a few days in each, sending back stories as he found them. He visited Burma and went on a jungle patrol in Malaya looking for terrorists. He flew next to Japan and then on to Korea to see the effects of the war on the people. They were all subjects that he had written about before, but he had felt the need to see things at first hand for himself. He finally flew back via Honolulu and New York, the place that fascinated him more than any other in the world. He managed to make at least one trip there every year from 1953 until his death in 1967. When he arrived back towards the end of January 1952 he found that Cecil King had become Chairman of the *Daily Mirror* in place of Bartholomew. This event had occurred a week after he had left on his trip.

Travel was an all-important stimulus to Bill Connor, possibly more so than to other journalists. He depended on it. Lee Howard, the present editor of the *Mirror*, says that Connor used travel as a way of 'recharging his mental batteries'. Anyone who spends his days churning out a column in the surroundings of four grey office walls has to get away. Not only did Connor depend on it; he thrived on it. He loved visiting new countries or revisiting old favourites. He was fascinated by people in their own surroundings. And he liked the glamour of travel, the passports, the airliners, and the strange-sounding names. On average he would spend something approaching two months of every year travelling abroad. The mileage he covered was impressive. Like most people who travel a lot he had a large collection of stories. One of his favourites occurred during one of his many visits to New York. He was flying there in a Boeing Stratocruiser—an airliner with four piston-engines. Shortly after they had taken off from Gander, after a re-fuelling stop, one of the engines stopped, and the captain's voice was heard over the loudspeaker explaining that there was nothing to worry about and that he'd switched off the engine 'in the interests of greater safety'. On hearing this, a voice from the back of the aircraft shouted out, 'Why not turn them *all* off then?'

The influence of travel showed up in the writings; the moment he had returned from abroad his column showed a renewed zest, a sharper edge, a keener look. And of course many of the columns that he wrote while he was abroad were among his best. Take, for example, his interview with the late Senator Joseph McCarthy, which was called 'Fun at the Dentist's', and was written in May 1953 during a visit to Washington.

I'm a bit short of sleep and to save anybody else asking me what Senator Joseph McCarthy is like and how do you set about seeing him I'll set it down in black and white. Then will you let me roll over and doze?

This is exactly how you do it.

You fly to New York and then you fly to Washington. You then pick up the telephone book, look up Senator Joseph R. McCarthy and ring him up in the Senate Office Building.

'May I speak to Senator McCarthy please?'

'Who is calling?'

You tell the sweet suave feminine voice and she says that the Senator is busy. Will you call later?

You will. You do.

This telephonic crane dance goes on for a couple of days. Will Miss Sweetness please place personally in front of the Senator a message to say that a man has come all the way from Europe to see him? Will she please tell Senator McCarthy to stop wasting my time, to stop wasting his time, to stop wasting his secretary's time, to stop wasting electricity on the telephone system and to tell me to clear off to Europe—which I will do with great speed and pleasure—or alternatively will he see me? Just a plain yes or no. Miss Sweetness says sure she'll be glad to tell the Senator, and she'll call me back.

Yes, the Senator will see me and will I please be at his office at midday. I get there. He keeps me cooling my heels. At last McCarthy comes out.

Can wickedness have charm? I think it can and in this stocky, dangerous, vastly ambitious man it seems to go hand in hand. Will I ride downtown with him in his car? Yes, but is this one of these squalid gabble-and-run occasions in which he can spare me only two or three minutes in a phoney American schedule-crammed day? McCarthy grins and says hell no.

He's going to the dentist and would I care to step right in? I told him that indeed I would, but perhaps it would be better to let him know right away that I detested everything he stood for, that I opposed what he was doing, and that on further acquaintance, I felt almost certain that I would hate his guts. Furthermore what the blazes was his idea in keeping me waiting in this sweaty town? The Senator from Wisconsin remarked thoughtfully that 'Jeez, this was straight shooting'.

We went into the surgery and McCarthy, still urbane and still slightly boyish, introduced me to Dr Stirling. This was a reporter from England. This was a straight shooter and Joe personally liked straight shooters. Would I have an anaesthetic? I said I'd have a double chloroform. The Senator said he'd have one too, and make it Scotch for both of us. McCarthy sat in the chair with the drink in his hand. I sat next to him.

I told the dentist that I dearly hoped he would hurt the Senator, and that if he thought this was a joke I was never more serious in my life. McCarthy grinned and said, 'See what I mean, doc?' I asked McCarthy if he knew that a total blockade of China would mean the downfall of Hong Kong and did he want to see bits of the Empire drop off like rotten apples?

He made a long rambling reply, the gist of which was that we were sending explosives to China under the guise of fertilizer which were killing American boys but he could sympathize with us if we saw our Empire falling apart.

I asked him what he thought of Cohn and Schine and he said that they were about their lawful business in Europe and what was all the fuss about? I told him we disliked little snoopers but that if he wished to drive a further wedge between the United States and Great Britain he should send Cohn and Schine back to England again and he would further damage Anglo-American friendship.

More Scotch was served.

The dentist drilled his teeth. The nurse, charming and attractive but also deeply impressed and honoured to have such a distinguished patient, fussed around. McCarthy lay there with his mouth wide open and as he was unable to talk, I asked him if I could tell him a funny story. He nodded.

I said that in Milan there is a square that is called the Piazza Loreto. In the Piazza there is a garage. Outside the garage there is a canopy, and supporting the canopy there is an iron girder. On the morning of 29 April 1945 there was a gentleman attached to the girder. He was suspended upside down by a rope. His mouth was very wide open—just like the Senator's—and the similarity, to me, was astonishing.

The name of the man was Benito Mussolini, and I wondered if dictators dead could look like would-be dictators alive.

Joe shut his mouth, and I think what could be called a shadow of pain clouded his face. The dentist looked as if a block-buster had hit him. The nurse sagged and appeared dazed. So I gave her what might be called a mirthless wink which, to my astonishment, she returned in an unhappy sort of way. I asked McCarthy to soothe the pair of them.

I said that there should be no cause for distress anywhere as it was clearly understood between McCarthy and myself that this was going to be a frank conversation of the type that formidable and powerful politicians could handle in their stride. Would the Senator therefore calm the dentist and put the nurse at her ease?

Mr McCarthy growled 'Relax'.

Order was not fully restored so I made what I thought was a helpful suggestion and indeed a social gesture. Would the dentist prescribe another anaesthetic and I personally did not care too much for ice with my Scotch?

Drinks were served.

The semi-electrocuted dentist went on with the filling and the nurse continued in her role as an attractive but astonished barmaid.

From the dentist's with all its corrosive jollification, we moved back to the Senate Office Buildings where the Senator indulged in a little verbal mayhem himself denouncing the British for killing American soldiers for the sake of commercial gain. The few odd calculations that I was able to make about blood spilt in two World Wars and treasures piled up in the second which made the United States easily the richest and most powerful nation on earth, made no impression on McCarthy. From the Senate Offices we moved to a house which he either owned or in which he was welcomed as a most favoured son.

I was now in the role of a violent extraordinary trophy that the Senator had brought home for his friends to see. He remarked that he had never seen anybody like me before and I replied that in his case neither had I, and hoped that it would never occur again.

A rancorous time was had by all, and after remarking that I hoped his teeth hurt for ever more, the fragrant encounter came to an end.

A violent article, with none of the usual thank-you-sir-for-seeing-me-a-humble-newspaperman courtesies. But also an inspired article, one which, bristling at every paragraph, showed how the stimulus of travel—'the re-charging of the batteries'—could work for Connor. And one which could well be counted among the best.

Bill Connor was well and truly back in the saddle.

CHAPTER SEVEN

THE FURIOUS FIFTIES

LOOKING at Bill Connor's career as a journalist with the full —and slightly dubious—wisdom of hindsight, it is possible to discern phases. The dividing lines are faint and probably a little arbitrary, but the periods are nonetheless interesting to look at. Even more fascinating is to try to give names to these various phases. For instance, one could call the first half-dozen or so years, from 1935 to the early part of the war, the Years of the Apprentice. The period from 1942 up to 1950 could well be Years of Battle—a battle both in the sense of a war and also one against frustration and unease afterwards. But the third period, the one that started round about 1951 and continued right up to 1960, is the difficult one. A name does not spring easily to mind for it —or at least, a name that does it full justice. These years were without doubt the most physically exacting ones for Connor. He lived hard, he worked hard and he travelled hard. His talents and abilities were used and taxed to the full. It was mentally invigorating—and physically exhausting. They were the years when his column began to be more than just another newspaper feature. Like a bird, he had already learned to fly—to write a good column—in the years before. But during the 1950s he learned to soar like an eagle. They were magnificent years, erratic years, expansive years. In the end they took their toll. Had he not driven himself so hard during this time, Connor might well have lived a while longer.

Looking at columns taken at random during the 1950s one senses a feeling of instability. Some days they were good, very good. Other days they were ordinary. And on yet other days they were bad, inordinately so. They were more extreme and less tempered than some of the later ones. They read as though they were written with the emotional taps turned full on. When they were vitriolic—which they often were during this period— they were *very* vitriolic. Blisteringly, punishingly so. Indeed, one of the most blistering ones landed Connor in court with a libel action brought against him and the *Daily Mirror* by the American pianist Liberace. The columns were hot and impetuous. And then there were others that appeared a little slapdash; or maybe they could have been directed at a better target, or a more worthy opponent. The quality of the articles written in the 1950s was higher than it had ever been, but the consistency was not.

For a brief while after the closure of *Public Opinion* in 1951 Bill Connor's career was rather quiet. He was writing a regular column and enjoying being solely a columnist once again. His round-the-world trip at the end of 1951 and the firing of Bartholomew had been significant events, but now there was a lull. Cecil King was finding his feet as the new Chairman, old faces were disappearing from the *Mirror* to be replaced by new ones. It was as if everyone was watching events and brooding on them but nobody wanted to act prematurely. Wait-and-see was the watchword; and Bill Connor was quite content to do just this.

1952 came and went. King George VI died. The newspapers heralded the new Elizabethan Age with great fervour. It was as though, at long last, all vestiges of the war and post-war period had been removed. People started to look to the future and stopped licking the physical and mental wounds that the war had left. The Labour Party were beginning their long exile—an exile during which they tried time and time again to tear themselves apart. Bill Connor continued writing steadily. The familiar spectacles at the top of his column looked down on the day's events. But still he was comparatively quiet. He travelled briefly to Rome, but nowhere else. He was about to break into the most exhausting phase in his life, but for the moment he rested.

In 1953 he began to emerge, to take the first steps towards being known and loved—and known and hated—all round the world. Until then his reputation had been made primarily in Britain. The events of 1953 and the years that followed were to extend that reputation. In May of that year he went again to America, first to New York and then down to Washington where he waited for two days for his interview with Senator Joseph McCarthy. The article resulting from that meeting—as has already been seen—was accounted a success. In October he returned to America and from there went on a trip round the paper mills which the *Mirror* owned in Canada. He wrote articles on the Coronation and on the Dockers—the gold-plated Daimler variety—who were regularly hitting the headlines. The *Mirror* published one of its 'Churchill must go' editorials—and Churchill stayed. Bill Connor had a letter from Lord Beaverbrook. It marked the start of an elaborate courtship by the Beaver, a wooing that went on for years. Beaverbrook had a very great regard for Connor's writing talent and was very keen to get him to come over to 'the sunny side of the street', to use his own phrase. Connor was flattered and tempted—not for the first time —but he did not go. Their correspondence was to continue up to the time of Beaverbrook's death in 1964.

And so to 1954. It was during this year that he wrote a number of profiles of important people—a series which showed that he was on the way to reaching his peak. His technique, as he explained in a letter to Gilbert Harding—one of his subjects—was remarkably uncomplicated:

> My technique is a very simple one. I hire a private room at some eminently respectable hotel and take the guest there for a couple of hours where we have martinis and photographs to begin with and then settle down to the scampi and unpleasantries. What about it?

For this series he interviewed Billy Graham, Charles Chaplin, Hugh Gaitskell, Adlai Stevenson, Lord Mountbatten and, of course, Gilbert Harding. He enjoyed these meetings immensely. For a change he was able to take a studied look at some of the people who make news and to get behind the public face and try to find out what made them tick. He had done comparatively little interview journalism before then and he quickly found that he liked it very much.

His interviewing technique was partly responsible for the success of the profiles. He tried whenever possible to disarm his subjects, to make them less aware of the fact that he was a newspaperman and therefore more forthcoming in their opinions and attitudes. His interview with Lord Mountbatten was typical of his tactics. Mountbatten was stationed as Commander-in-Chief of the Mediterranean Fleet in Malta. He was about to be appointed First Sea Lord at the Admiralty. He had been sent a signal from the Admiralty which said that the *Daily Mirror* wanted to send Bill Connor out to find out what the Mediterranean Fleet thought of him and his appointment.

Mountbatten was not particularly keen to be investigated but, feeling that Connor was likely to do an honest job, he agreed to the request.

When Connor arrived in Malta he was greeted by one of Mountbatten's staff and invited to have a meal or a drink at Admiralty House. Connor declined the invitation and went off on a tour of the dockside bars to find out from the sailors what they thought of Mountbatten. Only after he had done that was he willing to meet Mountbatten personally.

His article, which was held over until April 1955 when Mountbatten was officially appointed First Sea Lord, was entitled 'Lord High, Wide and Handsome'. This is part of what he had to say:

> I visited the bars as well as Admiralty House in Malta and talked to the matelots about him.
>
> Were they in favour of Mountbatten? They put down their glasses with a questioning stare. 'Was I by any chance referring to Lord High, Wide and Handsome?'
>
> Is Blackpool in favour of Stanley Matthews? Is Northampton in favour of Tyson?
>
> I got the point.

Mountbatten and Connor talked for a long while of their various wartime experiences and their opinions of many of the national figures. Mountbatten found Connor's opinion refreshing and often highly entertaining.

The following year Connor made two major journeys abroad. The first was to America—yet again—where he interviewed Adlai Stevenson and Marilyn Monroe. He asked her if she knew any English people in Hollywood. She replied that she was a friend and admirer of Edith Sitwell; Connor was fascinated:

> This, I think is one of the finest juxtapositions I have ever heard of. I also think it is a genuine friendship. On the left we have Marilyn, the girl who, when asked: 'What do you think of sex?' replied: 'I

never give it a second thought.' On the right we have the Gothic
Edith Sitwell—one of the most formidable, wise, witty, terrifying,
antique and seasoned women in the world.
Marilyn likes Edith.
Edith likes Marilyn.
And I believe the pair of them.

Connor was much taken with Marilyn Monroe and found the
girl he described as the 'glint in every man's eye' very mixed up,
mournful and pleasing.

It was during this visit to the United States that Bill Connor
first met another of the eccentrics he so loved to collect. This time
it was the resplendently named Lucius Beebe, a millionaire who
owned a newspaper called the *Territorial Enterprise* (for which
Mark Twain had written), as well as an enormous St Bernard
dog named Mr T-Bone Towser. He was also a fine journalist
himself, writing for the *San Francisco Chronicle* and *Holiday*
magazine. Beebe lived in Virginia City, Nevada, an old ghost
silver mining town. He was a man who hated the so-called
advances of civilization. He distrusted the telephone, loathed
television and referred to aircraft as 'those tin cylinders of death'.
He wanted everyone to return to the old days when the West
really was Wild. He had been born a hundred years too late, but
that did not stop him trying to make amends for it. He always
wore a vast Stetson and carried silver dollars as his loose change.
He had his own private railway carriage full of Edwardian plush
and elegance. He also had a great passion for Rolls-Royce motorcars, owning many of them, usually coloured maroon and yellow
with wickerwork panels on the sides. And it was concerning a
Rolls-Royce that Beebe sought Connor's help. In June 1955 he
wrote to Connor:

Dear Bill,
    Can you do a little international spying for me, the fruits of which
I do not believe will imperil the Commonwealth or contribute to the
spread of alarm and despondency.
    The Rolls-Royce people, confronted by a potential customer for
one of their new cars, are running true to form. Their product is
hardly ever for sale and, in the event of the ultimate catastrophe, the

actual purchase of a car, delivery may not be looked for in the fore-
seeable future. Of course, the purchaser may not have the colour he
wishes, nor is he allowed any latitude of choice in gear shifts. He'll
bloody well take the hack the way Conduit Street wants him to have
it, disc wheels, low headroom and all. And a capacious boot. And
next year at the earliest.

Well, I've learned that the virtue or merit in owning a Rolls is not
the possession of the property but the achievement of its procuring,
always against the every instinct and inclination of the manufacturer.
It's a sad day at Crewe when an order really comes through.

One thing I do really want to know, and against my knowing of
which the entire organization of Rolls-Royce, from the managing-
director to the sergeant on the door, are urgently inhibited, is this: is
the motive power of the new Silver Cloud greater than that of the
Silver Dawn? A cabled enquiry by the San Francisco agency for Rolls
to the home office actually received the one word reply: 'Sufficient'.

Nobody is going to know the power rating of Rolls-Royce if the
management can help it. Least of all the purchaser. The very notion
is impudent.

Have you any friends you can blackmail into revealing this
mystery? I don't want a preview of the Holy Grail or a lease on
immortality; not even the Crown Jewels or an invitation to a royal
garden party; just the power potential in horsepower of the Rolls-
Royce Silver Cloud motor.

Connor's attempts to find out the horsepower of the car met
with dismal failure. Beebe gave up trying and simply bought one
to find out. He was well satisfied.

Beebe was powerfully in favour of alcohol, saloons, good food,
elegantly riotous living and gambling. His suggestion for longevity
was a beautifully simple one: just keep on breathing. One of his
greatest successes as a crusading newspaper proprietor was when
he battled against the introduction of automatic dial telephones
in Virginia City. The battle was won and the victory was heralded
in the *Territorial Enterprise* with the succinct headline: 'PROGRESS
SUCCESSFULLY AVERTED.' His reason for taking up the challenge
in the first place was typical of the man. He believed that the old-
fashioned conscientious switch-board operator could allow a man
to stay drinking in his favourite saloon for days on end and had
enough sense not to bother him with frivolous calls from his wife.

Beebe fulfilled all Connor's requirements for an eccentric. He was larger-than-life, with an incomparable zest for living. He was rich and yet enjoyed his money in a very un-serious way. Money was a convenience to Beebe; it just made living the way he did a little easier. He was very witty—and, in an impish way, wise as well. Rules of ordinary behaviour were, to him, targets —to be shot at and to be broken as often as possible. Connor found him very entertaining and convivial company.

In addition to travelling to America, Bill Connor went to South Africa in 1955. He went with a small party of British journalists who wished to see for themselves the effects on the people of the apartheid policy pursued by the South African government. He found it odious and a total affront to human dignity. While he was there he met—for the first time—Father Trevor Huddleston (now the Bishop of Stepney). For much of his life Connor had had a suspicion of pontificating priests; he distrusted the academic cleric. Huddleston—like Billy Graham the year before—he found to be the complete antithesis. He liked and admired the tall, immensely charming priest. He was full of admiration for the man's courage, for he was disliked intensely by the white government and many of the coloured South Africans viewed him with deep suspicion. He walked round the Sofiatown area with Father Huddleston. Faces—and not all of them friendly—peered from the shadows everywhere they went. Connor wrote of 'the smell of fear' of the place. He later admitted that he had personally been very afraid while they had been walking about Huddleston's parish. He had been very glad to have Huddleston with him.

This was the first of a number of meetings with Huddleston. Connor got on very well with him. As well as his completely practical and humanistic approach to religion, Connor liked Huddleston's rebel nature, a characteristic which has at times got him into disfavour with more than just the South African government. Connor felt that Huddleston was a man who cared much more for his people than for his bishops, and by Connor's reckoning that was just what any priest should do. After Huddleston was thrown out of South Africa they met again in England, and then later when Huddleston was Bishop of Masasi,

Connor, on yet another of his trips, spent Easter with him. Huddleston remembers Connor saying to him, on his arrival at Masasi: 'I thought that as I was covering the Eichmann trial in Jerusalem I might as well come on and visit you.'

In September of 1955 Connor and his family went to the South of France for a holiday. While they were staying in St Tropez, a very large yacht, the M.S. *Shemara*, came into the harbour. Sir Bernard and Lady Docker, who were holidaying on the Riviera, had heard that he might be there and had brought their boat along to see. A big crowd of curious bystanders collected on the quay to watch. They were even more surprised when a large, bespectacled Englishman detached himself from amongst them and gave a great piercing whistle and yelled: 'Hello, ducks!' to the Dockers as they stood on deck. Bill Connor was greeting his friends. The onlookers were even more surprised when, later that afternoon, the same fat Englishman dived off the side of the boat into the harbour for a bet. Since the yacht is no tiddler, the dive was fairly spectacular.

On their way home the Connors went to stay for a few days with Charlie Chaplin who had invited Connor when he had been interviewed by him the year before. The public Charlie Chaplin is extremely well-known. The private one is even more likeable. The man has genius, not just as an actor and comedian, but as the head of a large, rambling, intensely likeable family. One evening he spent hours entertaining everyone with a one-man version of 'Limelight', the film that he had just completed at that time. He acted out most of the parts and played the music. The phrase 'home entertainment' takes on an entirely new meaning when Chaplin is doing the entertaining.

One of the things about America that deeply interested Connor was its political system. To a foreigner it is, without doubt, one of the strangest imaginable. How it works, no one really knows, but, against all rules of common sense, it does. And Connor became a proper student of it in 1956 when he attended both Party Conventions, the Democratic one in Chicago and the Republican one in San Francisco. His guide was Ralph Champion, head of the *Daily Mirror*'s New York office and an old friend. They attended all the ballyhoo and barely-controlled

mayhem together. Connor was amazed. He had never seen anything like it before. The shouting, the cheering, the balloons and
paper hats and badges and finally the selection of the Presidential
candidates—all were astounding to him. It was an experience that
so intrigued him that he repeated it twice more at later dates.

But there was one event of 1956 that was to affect Connor much
more than the idiosyncrasies of the American political system.
In September the American pianist Liberace came to Britain to do
a tour. He was greeted with hysterical enthusiasm by his fans. A
special train brought him from Southampton to Waterloo. His
arrival was reported in all the newspapers—after all, it made a
good story. Bill Connor decided that he would write a piece on the
arrival of Liberace. This he duly did. As Hugh Cudlipp said in his
book *At Your Peril*, '. . . they were undoubtedly the most
expensive [words] William Connor ever wrote'. Liberace
successfully sued him for libel. He was awarded £8,000 in
damages plus £27,000 in legal costs. The case achieved far
greater public attention than the words that had brought it about.
In America it was christened 'The Liberace Show' by *Time*
magazine; in England the *Guardian* called it the 'case of the year'.
It was remarkable, not only for the amount of hilarity it provoked
inside the court as well as out, but also for the masterly display
of Liberace's prosecuting counsel Gilbert Beyfus, Q.C. It was
almost his last big case and 'The Old Fox' certainly lived up to his
name.

If 1956 was an explosive year for Connor, 1957 went, literally,
with an even bigger bang. In May he travelled to Christmas
Island in the eastern part of the Indian Ocean to observe the
exploding of Britain's second hydrogen bomb. It was perhaps
the single most chilling sight that Connor ever witnessed—and he
saw quite a lot. He wrote about it in a column which he called
'Like an oil painting from Hell':

> At forty-nine minutes past ten on the 31st day of May in the Year
> of Our Lord 1957, in the neighbourhood of Christmas Island, named
> after Him, the British people exploded their second hydrogen bomb.
> It was a dress rehearsal for the death of the world.
> Standing on the rolling deck of H.M.S. *Alert* and clad in white

protective clothing with hoods and goggles, we, the observers, looked like grotesque mourners.

High overhead, at a height of what was probably eight miles, a Valiant bomber painted all-white sped at over 600 miles an hour to the firing point. In its sleek belly was the bomb, known to one and all on Christmas Island as 'The Beast', but politely referred to by the scientific director in charge as 'a nuclear device'.

We were thirty-five miles from where The Beast was due to explode after being spewed out from the bomber—quite near enough in view of the fact that the power of the bomb was equal to several million tons of T.N.T.

I waited with feelings of excitement, awe and a faint sense of horror. The ship's loudspeakers broke into an iron, throaty, roar as a giant voice began to count downwards to Moment Zero.

Forty, thirty-nine, thirty-eight, thirty-seven . . .

It was like the footsteps that lead to the execution shed. We had our backs turned away from the bursting point. . . .

Eighteen, seventeen, sixteen . . .

We were invited to cover our closed eyes with our hands. The Beast was plummeting down in a great deadly arc . . .

Four, three, two, one . . . FIRE!

Through closed eyes, through dark glasses and with my hands still covering my face, I saw the flash. Brighter than the sun, hotter than the sun and ripped out of the secrets of the heart of the Universe.

Still with our backs to the burst, we remained there for another fifteen seconds before we were allowed to turn round and open our eyes.

AND THERE IT HUNG BEFORE US: A BOILING RED AND YELLOW SUN LOW ABOVE THE HORIZON. IT WAS AN OIL PAINTING FROM HELL. BEAUTIFUL AND DREADFUL. MAGNIFICENT AND EVIL.

The golden whirling ball changed colour . . . from orange and grey . . . to a light muddy purple.

It then re-formed and became a bloated top-heavy Christmas pudding, with a greyish, whitish sauce, streaming out of the top and spilling down at the sides like a filthy lava. The shock waves could be seen feathering out in a scimitar shape, and the grunt and thump of the blast hit us—not sharply but as a dinghy nudges when it hits the shore.

The men around me were too quiet, and in a blasphemous way it reminded me of the silence that was once so poignant a memory of Armistice Day on November 11.

We were watching something also connected with death on a prodigious scale—death, however, that does not lie in the past but death that is waiting in the future.

The vast shape, now increasing in size every moment, rose upward and turned with a reddish glow in the interior. A thin, snake-like stem appeared at its base, as steam and water were sucked up from the sea below. The horrible pudding in the sky became a diseased cauliflower then changed into the familiar mushroom.

Mr W. J. Cook—the brilliant scientific director who is not only the stage manager and producer but also the part author of this grim and terrifying performance—was at great lengths to emphasize the safety of the nuclear device from the point of view of 'fall-out'.

In his precise and academic manner he became almost enthusiastic about the odds of anyone in the Pacific and in Australia and Japan and the United States, suffering any after-effects from this almost—as it seemed—hygenic weapon.

But, with my hands over my eyes, wrapped from head to foot in protective clothing and wearing a device to detect excessive radiation, I couldn't help thinking of the real power of The Beast.

The flash, crash and roar of the hydrogen bomb set off in the most remote and desolate part of the world is a source of wonderment and, indeed, of pride to some people like Lord Cherwell.

But when released over cities where it would obliterate millions of men, women and children in a trice, it is a wicked, an evil thing.

There is one story that arose from this look at naked terror which throws an interesting sidelight on Bill Connor. The actual test had been postponed a number of times so that it finally fell on a Saturday. This meant that the various daily newspaper correspondents would have difficulty in sending their stories to catch their deadlines. The Press Officer therefore made arrangements for those who wanted to to send their pieces before the actual detonation (stories are very often written in advance). Connor, however, chose not to. The consequence was that most other daily newspapers got their stories before the *Mirror* did. The *Mirror* people were very angry—they had missed out slightly. What they did not realize was that Connor preferred to write his piece on what he had actually seen and not on what the correspondents had been told they would see. He duly filed his copy after the explosion. He never let on that he had been the only daily newspaperman to write his piece on what he had seen. He just accepted the anger of the *Mirror* without saying a word in defence of his action.

In a less sombre vein, Connor flew down to Plymouth to watch the departure of the replica of the Pilgrim Fathers' ship the *Mayflower* shortly before he went to Christmas Island. While he was there he was shown round the tiny ship by the captain, Alan Villiers. 'Rather you than me,' was his comment on seeing just how small it was. Later on, in June, he was in America to watch the arrival of the ship at Cape Cod. It had sailed some three and a half thousand miles in the time he had taken to travel once round the world.

During 1957 Connor had become interested in a certain Father Borelli, who ran a special kind of orphanage in Naples called the House of Urchins. In December of that year he flew to Naples to take a look at this extraordinary priest who helped the abandoned children of that dead-end city. Connor was completely won over by what he saw. He found the children—'the human rubbish of Naples, born in misery and sin'—delightful. Through the efforts of Father Borelli and his helpers they had retrieved a little of their self-respect. They had an evening meal—usually nothing more than a bowl of greasy soup, a big hunk of dry bread and a piece of cheese—and beside each child was a little square of cloth 'that stood for a serviette . . . a brave little flag of tattered elegance that stood for civility and self-respect'. But what really astounded him was that the House of Urchins existed entirely on the meagre contributions that came to it from all over the world from the boys themselves who, when they are fourteen, try to find work and contribute a third of any money they earn to the general good. As Connor said at the end of the article he wrote after his visit: '. . . Father Borelli, and the good priests who help him, are fighting a fight with compassion as their sword and kindness as their shield. The smile on the faces of the children of the House of Urchins is their flag of victory.' Connor had found yet another example of a practical priest. As a result of his article appearing in the *Daily Mirror*, some £600 was sent to him from readers all over the country to be donated to these children.

During 1958—and the following year—Bill Connor did less

travelling than in previous years. The reason for this was simple; he and the *Daily Mirror* were preparing their defence of the Liberace libel. It was rather like an army preparing a defensive position. They were digging themselves in, and hoping to make themselves a little more protected against the onslaught that was to come. A case of the size of this one always entails an enormous amount of preparation and legal work. The exact words complained of have to be designated. Answers to each of them have to be ready. For months before, Connor was spending two or three hours a day with the legal advisers of the *Daily Mirror* going over every imaginable aspect of the case. But even this extraordinary amount of work did not prevent Connor from making another notable journey abroad.

In mid-January 1958 he travelled to Italy and then to Greece where he had an interview with Archbishop Makarios. Makarios was at that time Head of the Church of Cyprus. Nine months before he had returned from the Seychelles, where he had been deported for a year by the British Government. Connor was interested in finding out what this 'bad man' now thought of the British. He found him a subtle, sensitive and deeply comprehending man. He liked him personally. He admired the man's 'intellectual horsepower'. Connor went on, in his article, to point out that 'the British have an unfortunate record when they imprison or deport their political opponents. Their victims have a habit of turning up again as Prime Ministers, like Mr Nehru, or Mr de Valera.' It was a Cassandra prophecy that turned out to be accurate. Makarios returned later in triumph to Cyprus and was appointed Prime Minister.

From Cyprus Connor flew to Turkey and then on to Israel. Here, with Sidney Jacobson, the *Mirror*'s Political Editor, he saw David Ben-Gurion, the Israeli Prime Minister. Ben-Gurion had the reputation of being a difficult man. Other journalists had tried to see him and failed, or had come away from seeing him with very little to show for it. Jacobson recalled their interview. They were shown into the Prime Minister's office. Jacobson started with some preliminary talk, in an attempt to break the ice a little. Connor then asked Ben-Gurion his first key question, the one on which the whole of the remainder of the interview depended. If it had been banal or stupid, no doubt their time with Ben-Gurion would have been sharply curtailed. He said: 'Was it worth the slaughter of six million Jews to strengthen the state of Israel?' Ben-Gurion's reply was: 'No—it wasn't,' and proceeded to explain why in great detail. He had been asked the right question, and the whole tone of the interview became more relaxed. The three of them talked for some time. A potentially difficult situation had been neatly and successfully avoided. Ben-Gurion's suspicions of foreign journalists had been allayed.

Connor took the opportunity, while he was in Israel, to look at two other sights he had not seen before—a kibbutz and the Holy Land. The kibbutz—a community of people who pool their skill and their labour for the common good—he found fascinating. Here were people who were carving a home and a living for themselves out of the roughest land. Deserts were being made, literally, to flower by scientific techniques, by courage and by fierce, grinding toil. But those same people were forced to carry guns as well as spades. They were near the Gaza Strip, where there was fighting at the time. Then, as now, they had two fights on their hands. One was against Mother Nature, the other against Arab hatred and terrorist activity. Connor wished them well. He wrote: 'The story of the new-born Israel is, I believe, the most massive achievement of the century.'

The Holy Land he found a little disillusioning. Nazareth, he reported, was a sizeable dusty town with Coca Cola signs everywhere. The Sea of Galilee looked like a more beautiful version of Ullswater. The room where the Last Supper was supposed to have been held looked to him faintly like a small annexe in the Alexandra Palace. King David's tomb he likened to something out of Drury Lane. But despite this Connor was entranced by Israel and the Israelis. He admired the indomitable spirit of the people and the often breathtaking beauty of the countryside. It was, he said later to a friend, one of the few countries he would have liked to live in when he retired.

And so to 1959. It was a momentous year for Bill Connor. It was the year in which he celebrated his fiftieth birthday. It was the year in which the libel case was finally heard. And it was the year when his health started to fail.

The day following his birthday, he wrote in his column:

I was fifty yesterday. I don't feel a day older than sixty and when I'm really on form, with every ounce of strength mustered and respiration clearly detectable by the mirror-to-the-lips method, I feel fifty-nine.

Being fifty is the age at which you can really settle in and enjoy predicting disaster. When you put your fingers together, stretch your legs and say with an air of finality: 'No good will come of it', the young folks really begin to listen. 'Rum old devil,' they say, 'but he's seen a thing or two in his time.'

From now on, so far as I'm concerned, not much good is going to come of anything and I shall survey the hopeless scene with expanding pleasure.

Connor then went on to say that he had done some research into the notable events that had occurred in the past on 26 April, his birthday, and had found to his dismay that there had been practically nothing of significance. 'April 26th is the day of utter nothingness. I don't suppose there is a bleaker festival.'

That his health was failing was not discovered until after the court case when he went into hospital for a minor operation and the usual blood test showed that he had developed diabetes. This was due almost entirely to the great strain under which he been living. The case, and the preparation for it, on top of an already overloaded work routine, triggered it off. He reported the fact shortly after the case. He told the story of the blood test:

. . . It seems that apart from the fact that I was wearing pyjamas it was medically difficult to tell me apart from a toffee apple; a one-man Tate and Lyle factory; a human Mr Cube; just a couple of yards of barley-sugar. Sir Syrup in person.'

The Liberace libel not only affected Connor's health; it also affected his writing. Before it, he had used adjectives like gun-shot; his columns were peppered with them. But afterwards he did not rely on them nearly as much. As a result his writing became much greater. The power was diverted into the thoughts and not expended solely on the words themselves. But it seems a hard way to have improved his work.

The Liberace case opened on Monday, 8 June 1959, at the Royal Courts of Justice. The Judge was Mr Justice Salmon, who some years before had gained the reputation of being a stern man after the Notting Hill Gate race riots, when he had handed out very stiff sentences to the worst of the offenders. Liberace's counsel was Gilbert Beyfus Q.C., perhaps one of the best barristers—and certainly the wiliest—that this country has seen for a long time. The *Daily Mirror* and Bill Connor—the two defendants—chose Gerald Gardiner Q.C. (now Lord Gardiner) as their champion. They were probably the two best lawyers available. The case at least did not lack for legal expertise.

The first day of the trial—it went on for seven days—was spent in the outlining of prosecution's case by Beyfus. He first gave a short résumé of Liberace's career up to the time that the libel took place. He then went on to read out Connor's article and point out the major complaint—that certain passages of it suggested that Liberace was homosexual. Liberace was then called to the witness box and cross-examined first by Beyfus and then by Gardiner. Slowly the drama was unfolding.

The second day opened with Liberace still being questioned by Gardiner. After that, his witnesses came to the stand and were examined one by one. They included George Melachrino, Cicely Courtneidge, Mantovani and Bob Monkhouse. The prosecution's case was finished by half-way through the third day. It was a formidable one, put skilfully and with great care by Beyfus, who was in great form, full of guile and high emotion. It is a strange fact of the English legal scene that many leading lawyers and judges have brothers who are actors. It must be that the two professions have much in common, an ability to assume all and every kind of emotion at will. Beyfus did not have a brother on the stage, but he more than made up for it with his own Thespian ability. He feigned outrage, surprise, hurt, disappointment and anger throughout the case with an ability that could surely have earned him as illustrious a career on the stage as he had in the courts of law.

But the real fun started on the fourth day of the case when Bill Connor was called to the witness box to give his testimony. He was first examined by Gardiner—almost the complete opposite

of Beyfus in his quiet, restrained, logical manner—and then was
cross-examined by Beyfus. Beyfus showed small mercy in his
questioning. It was fast and furious and very rugged. He realized
that in Connor he had a powerful adversary and was determined
to discomfit him in whatever way he could. He was rude, he was
hectoring, he laid deep and complicated traps for Connor. But
Connor was like the cricketer who relishes fast bowling. Some of
the questions were turned aside with a neat verbal leg glance;
others were hit right out of the ground. Beyfus was in full flight
with his dramatic utterings and prancings—but so was Connor.

At one point in the cross-examination Beyfus was questioning
Connor on his reputation as a forceful writer:

> *Beyfus:* I want to ask you this question; do you think you have
> never appreciated the danger of words?
> *Connor:* Mr Beyfus, I used to be a close student of a paper called
> *Völkischer Beobachter* run by Dr Goebbels and I knew then and I know
> now what happens when words are wrongly used, when propaganda
> machines are used as in that case.

A little later on, Beyfus was quoting to Connor from a chapter
that had been written about him and his ability as a writer in
Hugh Cudlipp's book *Publish and Be Damned*:

> *Beyfus:* Your close colleague and superior, Mr Cudlipp, says that
> you remember every point of detail to the slightest disadvantage of
> the victim you pick up on the tip of your pen for public scrutiny in
> your column. 'When memory fails and the enormity of a politician's
> early misdemeanour temporarily escapes him, Cassandra taps his head
> and says: "My private librarians are looking it up." The value of the
> man is that he writes superbly, is a born journalist, means what he
> writes and writes without fear.'
> *Connor:* I would like you to read that again. I rather like that.
> *Beyfus:* I am sure you do . . .

Time and time again, as Beyfus and Connor were engaged in
their sparring, the court rocked with laughter. It was apparent that
most of the leading figures of the case were enjoying themselves—

if any enjoyment can be said to be had from a major legal case. This, quite naturally, presented its problems. Connor, as one of the two defendants, had to remain straight-faced for fear of being regarded, by the jury in particular, as irresponsible. Any such suggestion would have lost the case immediately. To keep a fighting chance the whole thing had to be regarded with a mock seriousness. But this could not prevent even the judge, Mr Justice Salmon, having a quiet chuckle.

One such incident occurred when Connor was being questioned about Liberace's arrival at Waterloo station and a particular event that occurred at that time when some women were kissing Liberace through the window of the railway carriage:

> *Beyfus:* You know quite well that no young girl kissed Mr Liberace?
> *Connor:* I remember looking . . .
> *Beyfus:* Would you look at the photograph? It is quite clear, is it not, that the young girl kissed the glass?
> *Connor:* I quite agree.
> *Gardiner:* He said through the window.
> *Beyfus:* Let me cross-examine, please.
> *Gardiner:* I do not think my learned friend heard the end of the answer. Mr Connor answers and lowers his voice at the end of his answers. He said she kissed through the window.
> *Beyfus:* I know. If I kiss someone through a window, I expect to kiss them. I do not expect to kiss a bit of glass.
> *Gardiner:* The lady apparently did it with the glass up.
> *Connor:* May we settle for a proximity of osculation?
> *Beyfus:* What a horrible word! One of the things that you told us caused you to write this article was a young woman kissing the glass of the carriage from the platform?
> *Connor:* Yes, indeed.
> *Beyfus:* And he put his lips to the corresponding part of the glass on the other side?
> *Connor:* That is right.
> *Beyfus:* You tell us you are married, but if you were a good-looking young man and you were unmarried, do you not think you would have done the same thing?
> *Connor:* My passion, though it always has been strong, has never forced its way through plate glass.

On the second day of his testimony Connor was in a far less ebullient mood than he had been. He was less willing to take on Beyfus at his own game. His answers were subdued and he left himself open to some very telling questioning. Whether it was the effect of the diabetes showing itself as lethargy or whether he had been told to curb his performance in the box, one cannot tell. But it is said that, had Connor—and some of his other witnesses—continued in the manner in which they started, the jury might have had a more difficult task in finding the libel proven.

In his closing speech, Mr Beyfus said:

'I was invited by my learned friend to try to match the language of Cassandra in my final speech to you. I do not think I can do it. He has put me on my mettle, but I am afraid that I cannot match him. But if this in any way resembles Cassandra, might I suggest that this newspaper is vicious and violent, venomous and vindictive, salacious and sensational and ruthless and remorseless? I do not think that is quite up to Cassandra's standards, but it is the best I can do.'

At this the court once again broke into laughter. It was the final witticism in a case more noted for its humour and classic displays of advocacy than for its finer points of law.

The jury were out for three and a half hours. On their return they declared that they had found the words complained of to be libellous and that the damages to be paid should be £8,000. It was a fair verdict.

There was one small event that occurred during the course of the trial that concerned Sir Thomas Beecham. After various witnesses had given evidence about the pianistic ability of Liberace, Beecham contacted Connor. Connor wrote about it in an obituary article in 1961:

> . . . I mourn him for many reasons. One of them is a personal regret that came from a missed but what might have been a great occasion. Eighteen months ago, I was involved (unsuccessfully on my part) in a tremendous public brawl in the Law Courts with a pianist named Liberace. . . . As this great piece of public entertainment moved towards its climax and various performers paid lavish tribute

to Mr Liberace's immense talent on the keyboard, it became known to me that Sir Thomas Beecham did not agree that the New Chopin in the Sequin Suit was a truly great artist. Alas, too late in the case, came a chance for Sir Thomas to have expressed his views strongly on my side. That would have been it. Maybe we would still have not won, but the last great horse-laugh, the final devastating load of witticisms might have crowned this uproarious case. A pity.

Liberace went home with his reputation intact; for a few brief weeks Connor's mail and his phone calls were full of congratulations and of abuse. The 75-year-old Beyfus lived a bare sixteen months more. Gerald Gardiner has gone on to far higher things. And Mr Justice Salmon still sits sagely on the Bench.

The 1950s—after the spectacular firework display of the libel case—came to a gentle close. Connor took his family to Italy for a holiday in September. While he was there he spent a week in Venice. He had spent many months there after the end of the war waiting to be demobilized and had many happy memories of that beautiful city.

Perhaps he was trying to recapture a little peace and a little quiet after the turmoil of the case. He was physically and mentally very tired, and was also having to learn to live with his diabetes. His eating and drinking habits—habits that had become set over a great number of years—were having to be changed. For almost the first time in his life he was having to listen to what the doctors said, even if he did not always take their advice.

Bill Connor, the fierce, fiery, vitriolic writer of the 1950s was undergoing a subtle change. Now aged fifty, he was beginning to mellow. His writing was becoming more powerful, more grandiose. He was beginning to realize that the rapier was every bit as effective a weapon as the club.

CHAPTER EIGHT

THE TRAVELLING TYPEWRITER

THE opening years of the 1960s witnessed an interesting phenomenon in Fleet Street. The *Daily Mirror* became 'respectable'. It was through no one episode or any conscious effort on the part of the paper. It just happened. It was as though people had decided in unison that that scandalous tabloid, that 'Labour rag', was not quite as awful as they had thought and that maybe it might be worth looking at after all. I remember a time, towards the end of the 1950s, when I was not allowed to read the *Daily Mirror* at school. It was not on the list of 'approved newspapers'—and I had to sneak out and buy my own copies. I found this very irritating, especially since it was the *Mirror* that was, indirectly, paying for me to be at the school.

This phenomenon was not restricted simply to the paper-reading public. Fleet Street itself was beginning to realize that the 'rumour-mongers' of Geraldine House were actually running a very fine newspaper—and quite a number of competitors began to look to the *Daily Mirror* as a textbook example of how a popular paper should be run. There was no longer any stigma to being the largest selling daily newspaper in the world. There was still the odd library or reading room that refused to have the *Mirror*, but they were the exceptions and not the rule.

Just as the paper became respectable, so did Bill Connor's column. A lot of people, whose reading had been hitherto confined to the fourth leader of *The Times* and a cursory glance at the *Tatler*, discovered that much of what Connor wrote in his column made sense to them. It was not uncommon to hear a voice in one or other of the more exclusive clubs say: 'Hello there, Charles. Seen what that Cassandra chappie's been on about today?'

Of course, the management under Cecil King and his deputy, Hugh Cudlipp, who had returned from his short stay with the *Daily Express* in 1953, had ambitious plans for the *Mirror*. King, in particular, wished to lose the 'rag' tag of the thirties and forties. The paper was being changed slowly and surely and this no doubt further helped it to become acceptable to a whole new group of people. But perhaps the other factor that helped—and doubtless the *Mirror* management of the time would disagree violently with this theory—is the fact that the important men on the paper, the men who wrote it, the men who edited it, who moulded it, who directed it, were getting older. The hard core of them had been there since the crazy days of the tabloid revolution in 1934–35. Then they had been men in their early twenties. Now they were men in their early fifties. The enthusiasm and boundless energy of youth were gone. The reckless, devil-may-care men of the middle 1930s were now middle-aged, tough, thoroughly experienced newspapermen. From being the bright young men of the pre-war period, they were, whether they liked it or not, becoming the father-figures of Fleet Street. Young journalists were arriving on the scene and talking about these men with—of all things—awe, and even respect.

Coupled with this fact was another—the generation gap. The war had, as with many other businesses, removed a large segment of men who would have been middle-management material at this period had they been alive. There were now, therefore, in nearly every newspaper office in London, senior men and juniors. The juniors were too junior to continue the madcap ways of their seniors. Their seniors were mellowing—and the papers with them.

Bill Connor reached the peak of his career in the 1960s. Just when, it would be invidious to say. He himself said, on more than one occasion, that he could never retire from writing his column; if he did, he said, it would mean losing the thread, and his own pride in his craft would not allow that. It is a small satisfaction, then, that he died while his writing was at its very best.

During the latter half of the 1950s Connor had increased the spectrum of his writing and had given it a truly world-wide compass. He had travelled a lot, had seen many of the important events throughout the world, and had talked to many of the world's leaders. This pattern continued during the 1960s.

Six days before his birthday in 1960, Connor flew to Russia with Bela Zola, a photographer from the *Mirror* and a close friend. The prologue to this is an interesting story in itself. Some time before, he had been in Paris to do a radio broadcast with a number of foreign newspapermen, including Alexei Adzhubei, Kruschev's son-in-law and editor of *Izvestia*. Connor complained to Adzhubei that he had always been refused a visa to visit Russia. He asked Adzhubei if it were at all possible to use his influence with Kruschev to help get a visa. The editor of *Izvestia* was most hurt and said that he would personally see to it that Connor was granted a visa and that there was no need to ask Kruschev at all. On his return from Paris Connor applied for a visa and was granted one immediately.

So it was, then, that Connor and Zola found themselves at Moscow Airport in late April, carrying amongst their luggage a typewriter, several cameras and film, ten pounds of English sausages and a box of kippers. The last two items were for British friends in Moscow, for whom such things were unobtainable. They were of course given the inevitable interpreter-cum-guide, to make sure they did not stray too far away from the official paths and see things they were not meant to see. From Moscow they went to Kiev, Kharkov, Sochi—the resort on the Black Sea—Tashkent (which Connor found the most beautiful of all the places they visited), Kuibyshev, Stalingrad and Leningrad. While Zola photographed everything that moved, Connor wrote a number of articles. The two of them attended a wedding in Leningrad in the Wedding Palace, where marriage is treated much as a production-line process, complete with canned music and a special 'Celebration Room' where the toast to the happy couple is drunk. Connor decided that, while he was about as far away as possible from anyone who might recognize him, he would grow a beard. He was horrified to discover that it was pure white. He shaved it off quickly. The two of them returned from Russia by way of Warsaw, since Connor's visa allowed him only one entry into Russia, and because he wished to see Poland. Zola managed to get a great number of photographs out of the country without having to hand them over to the authorities for censorship by the simple expedient of winding them all back into their cassettes and pretending they were unused. Much of this photographic material was used in the book that Connor wrote on his return.

Connor stopped only about eight weeks in England on his return from Russia. Then he packed his bag again and went to America for his, by now, annual trip. This time he had a specific purpose in mind. There was another presidential election coming up in October and he wanted to attend the two Party conventions. He travelled to Los Angeles for the Democratic one, at which John F. Kennedy was nominated and then to Chicago, where Richard Nixon was made the Republican candidate. Michael King—son of Cecil King, and the *Mirror*'s Foreign Editor—accompanied him, as did Ralph Champion of the *Mirror*'s New York office. Because of the astounding number of people who always attend these conventions King and Connor found themselves sharing a hotel room in Los Angeles. King remembers one little incident from this trip. The two of them had checked into their hotel and had gone to their room for a wash and to get changed for dinner. As they left their room to go downstairs, Michael King switched off the light. Connor thereupon switched it on again. King was a little puzzled and asked him why he wanted the light on. Connor replied: 'Look, they're charging us 50 dollars a day for this room. I just want to make sure we're getting our money's worth.'

With the two contestants for the Heavyweight Contest of the West settled and getting nicely into training, Connor flew home again. When he got back he wrote to Arthur Schlesinger, a member of Kennedy's staff whom he had met at a conference on journalism at the University of Missouri the previous year. He wanted to try to fix an interview with Kennedy, whom he believed would be the winner in the autumn. Kennedy was too busy, but Connor was given to believe that he might be able to see him after the election.

Connor returned to America in October in time to see Nixon beaten for the presidency by a close—or not-so-close—shave. Kennedy had won—and was to bring a brand new kind of diplomacy to Washington. Connor took the opportunity of being in Washington to remind his advisers that an interview had been promised.

The following year the *Daily Mirror* moved out of their offices in Geraldine House to the great 'Palace of Pain' (as it was known to many of its habitués) at Holborn Circus. It was a bigger, more splendid, brasher building than that of any other newspaper, and fitting and tangible evidence that the *Daily Mirror* was the most successful paper of the day.

In March 1961 Bill Connor set out on a long trip round the Middle East and East Africa. He flew first to Nairobi and then to Masasi where he spent Easter with Trevor Huddleston. While he was there he also went to see C. J. P. Ionides, the 'Snake Man'. Ionides was another eccentric for Connor to add to his collection. He made his living catching snakes and sending them to all parts of the world for medical research and for zoos. Ionides had lived in the then Tanganyika for thirty-six years and did not appear to be at all surprised when Connor arrived and said he had come to see the art of snake-catching. Ionides took Connor out and showed him how it was done. As they were driving back with their catch, a native stepped out of the bush and asked them for a lift in the Land-Rover. Ionides said: 'Ah, the folly of mankind! A car obviously loaded to the gunwales with men and serpents, yet he asks to come aboard.' Connor found Ionides to be very likeable, fearless and philosophical: 'A man very much after my own heart is C. J. P. Ionides —snakes and all.'

Connor then flew back to Israel to be present at the trial of Adolf Eichmann in Jerusalem. The Israelis had taken great care with their prisoner, first in catching him and then in making sure that he lived to be tried. Security procedures were very stringent outside and inside the court. Anyone entering the room where the trial was being held was searched very thoroughly. But this was the most dramatic part of the case. Connor was surprised at the ordinariness of it all. This is what he wrote:

The time is six minutes to nine o-clock in the morning. The place is the court-room of the community centre in Jerusalem. A side door opens and Adolf Eichmann walks into his bullet-proof armour-plated dock.

So this is the man who, if the charges are proved against him, will be by far the greatest killer in the history of mankind. Compared with him Genghis Khan was a welfare worker.

What does Eichmann look like? The appearance is that of a rather severe country solicitor who might well be on the board of governors of the local hospital.

The lips are thin, the hair is sparse, the nose beaky and the complexion sallow. He wears a dark, neat suit, a white shirt and a spotted tie. There is an air of respectability about him.

Three judges enter and all stand. Eichmann bows very slightly towards Supreme Court Judge Landau, who at once begins to read the tremendous indictment.

In its scale it is almost incomprehensible. The mind just cannot grasp what is being laid at this man's door.

The scenes of horror cover twenty-one countries reaching from the steppes of Russia to the tiny State of Monaco. The work of this man, this creature, penetrated throughout the whole of Europe with the exception of the British Isles and Spain—and we may count ourselves lucky.

Death was his business and he knew it well.

Adolf—son of Adolf Karl Eichmann, as he is rather ceremoniously styled in this court—is accused of causing the death of six million Jews, of torture, of starvation, of oppression, of overcrowding, of enslavement, of persecution, of deportation, of causing mental harm, of terrorist methods, of sterilization.

As the hideous catalogue of evil is read out to him—first in Hebrew, then in German—his face remains completely impassive. There is nothing unusual about him, except that he stands oddly and bends slightly backwards. The accusations take seventy-three minutes to read and translate before his counsel, Dr Robert Servatius, rises.

The Doctor is markedly Teutonic in appearance, with a massive head that rises straight from the back of his collar. He speaks slowly and deliberately.

I have the impression that out of Dr Adenauer's Germany has come a strong defender of what most people think is the impossible.

At once he challenges the constitution of the court. This is an excellent, if obvious, tactic. He immediately questions the right of one of the three judges on the grounds of prejudice and lack of authority.

Eichmann himself has obviously not been ill-treated. He has been scrupulously well cared for, for the overwhelmingly good reason that at this moment he is a most precious human being to Israel— and although they may make him a corpse in a few months' time, they want him alive, alert and well, to play his terrible part in the demonstration that one man in the base and bestial Nazi regime could murder six million of his fellow men.

The Commandant of Jerusalem, Colonel Rossolio, who had been responsible for the custody of Eichmann for a year, told me yesterday that when the prisoner first arrived in Israel he seemed almost relieved that his wanderings and his flight had ended, but that a note of anxiety at the prospect of what might be in store for him became apparent later.

Eichmann was always scrupulously polite and stood to attention when spoken to. There was no tendency towards suicide, as far as his gaolers could see, but they were taking no chances. He was utterly unemotional, had not the slightest trace of humour, and did not ask for spiritual solace.

When the team of psychiatrists had finished with him 'it was', said Colonel Rossolio, 'they who felt they had gone nuts'.

Eichmann was amenable to his guards, who have been specially chosen as not having been bereaved or connected with the atrocities of the concentration camps.

He was obviously an able man or he would never have been able to run the enormous and monstrous organization that led to genocide. It was a vast machine and could not have been controlled except by an extremely competent man.

The only time Eichmann showed some slight feeling was when he heard Schubert or Mozart being played on the radio that belonged to his guards.

I can see him as I write these words. A thin trim man who at this moment is, through his lawyers, complaining that he cannot bring witnesses to Israel to give evidence for him as they would not be given safe conduct.

There was not much safe conduct for the Jews at the hands of Germany between 1935 and 1945.

Not much safe conduct in the gas ovens.

Not much safe conduct for the women and babies machine-gunned in the communal graves and pits.

It is odd that all the maniacal madness of mankind gone berserk should be symbolized in the physical person of one who would go unnoticed at a church service in Balham.

At the end of the trial Eichmann was found guilty and later hanged.

IC

In July Bill Connor flew to Berlin. Here he interviewed Herr Willy Brandt, at that time the Mayor of Berlin. The Communists had just erected the Berlin Wall, cutting the city in two and dividing the two German people even more viciously. Connor wanted to know what Brandt and the West Berliners thought of this evil deed.

Connor then went to the Labour Party conference in Blackpool and after taking a short holiday in Ireland, flew to America for his promised interview with President Kennedy at the White House. This is part of what he wrote.

> I have been talking alone in the White House with President Kennedy of the United States. The procedure of admittance to this lovely building in the heart of Washington was slightly odd. At the gate on Pennsylvania Avenue the guard, a most genial fellow, asked me to produce some evidence that I was me and that me was I—such as a driving licence, a passport, a letter, a hotel bill—anything.
>
> I had nothing.
>
> I might have been a clean-shaven Castro for all they knew. He grinned affably and said: 'Better go up to the House and try your luck.'
>
> I said: 'It will be too bad if I have to open fire to prove the cordial spirit of Anglo-American friendship.'
>
> He replied in a mock English accent: 'That wouldn't be cricket, old chappie.'
>
> The President looks astonishingly young—even younger than his forty-four years. . . .
>
> . . . There is no doubt that this most pleasant man carries the greatest burden in the world. The responsibilities of this youthful Atlas are greater than Kruschev's—for the President has to serve and to please a free people and has anything but a free hand. . . .

Connor asked President Kennedy if he thought that world tension—especially over the Berlin crisis—had increased the possibility of war. Kennedy thought that this was not necessarily so, and went on to point out that an all-out conflict in Vietnam could radically change this situation of armed stalemate, and was therefore to be avoided.

> Mr Kennedy seemed very conscious of the world-wide liabilities and responsibilities of the United States to hostile pressures from the Soviet Union at many points.

Connor was a little worried by an impression he gained while at the White House that Kennedy was not at that point in direct control of the day-to-day situation in Berlin and that some military figure could easily make a fatal blunder. (This interview was, of course, shortly before Kennedy's famous 'Ich bin ein Berliner' speech, a speech that showed his real strength as the leader of the Western world.)

Connor concluded his report of the interview with these words:

> The President's popularity is increasing every day.
>
> The main reason—which I well understand after talking to him privately—is sympathy for him. Sympathy that so young a man should bear such a prodigious burden. Sympathy that such an attractive and intellectually sensitive figure should be confronted with such hideous problems. Sympathy with an idealist confronted with the greatest danger that mankind has ever known.
>
> But the harsh fact remains that the realities of brutal power politics cannot be erased by sympathy, and that an older and more experienced man might be a better occupant of the lonely place in the White House.

Kennedy's handling, not only of the Berlin crisis but also of the far more dangerous Cuban one, more than allayed Connor's spoken fears.

Connor's article did not go unnoticed by the White House entourage though not for the reasons one might have expected. They were quite happy about Connor's favourable—if slightly hesitant—impression of President Kennedy. But somewhere along the line their protocol feathers got ruffled. The *Daily Mirror*, in giving publicity on its front page to the fact that Connor had seen Kennedy, said that he had been alone with the President for over an hour. It also took out of the article—and reprinted them on the front page—two quotes which appeared to be hostile towards Kennedy. Arthur Schlesinger, the President's Special Assistant and the man who helped fix up the interview, wrote a very forcefully worded letter to Connor pointing out that the interview had not been exclusive to the *Mirror*, as was claimed, and that in any case, the 'ground rule for all such meetings is that, while the story may render the President's views in indirect discourse, it cannot say that the author actually met with the President'. This slightly puzzling rule had been broken, and Connor and the *Daily Mirror* duly apologized.

While he was in America Bill Connor took the opportunity to write an article on the John Birch Society, a strongly right-wing organization which had much in common with Senator Joseph McCarthy's political beliefs, another article on the Black Muslims, and a third article on the Rand Corporation. This is a non profit-making corporation of scientists, formed by the United States Air Force after the war. It has immense resources, and is said to have some of the finest technical brains in the United States. It includes some extraordinary people who publish long studies on such subjects as 'The Delicate Balance of Terror', and among them, a strong school of thought that urges getting the nuclear blow in first. Connor, as an old student of the more frightening elements of power politics, was interested in seeing these 'apostles of instant total destruction'.

Connor arrived back from America in mid-November, just in time to grab a clean shirt and a change of socks before flying East to spend Christmas with his ship. 'His' ship was H.M.S. *Cassandra*, and he had been adopted by the ship's company as their mascot a couple of years before. They had invited him out to Singapore. He was delighted to accept, and duly joined them three days before Christmas. It was a return match for a ball which had been organized by the *Mirror* for the ship before she was commissioned in 1960. Connor sent back a dispatch on this naval engagement which has somehow mysteriously managed to escape the official historian of the Royal Navy. He wrote:

Out here in this sweaty and booming town there is one of Her Majesty's ships by the name of *Cassandra*. Also out here is one of Her Majesty's subjects—again under the name of Cassandra. Last night both parties went into joint action to celebrate the advent of Christmas.

I came here at the invitation of Commander Spencer Drummond to make sure that all who sail under the flag and name of the original Greek prophetess of woe and disaster should have a thundering good time as the Eve of Christmas approaches. In short, we did.

Just about 200 Cassandrites—I think it may have been two or three pintfuls more—assembled here in the Armada Club at the Naval Base.

Christmas at home in Britain, is, by iron tradition, a matter of snow, of holly, of red berries, of Old Santa with his beard and cloak and loaded sack. Also Good King Wenceslas with his page and white stuff deep and crisp and even all around.

Out here, just 70 miles north of the Equator? No snow. No holly. No red berries. And only the damp enfolding heat—about 84 degrees right at this moment.

But in company with all the lads of H.M.S. *Cassandra* we did old Santa proud.

This ship, the ship you taxpayers bought and still maintain, this ship that My Lords of the Admiralty run—and damn you MY ship —has been out here in the Far East for more than two years now.

There was a break recently when our ship, their ship, your ship, MY ship had to belt off at about 23 knots to look after the trouble that suddenly flared up off Kuwait.

When it was cold there on board H.M.S. *Cassandra* in those Arabian waters, the temperature lurked around 105 degrees. When it was hot—well, it was as hot as hell.

Last night here in Singapore, as the evening baked on, it got a bit warm too.

At 7.30 sharp at this most excellent N.A.A.F.I. club the lads marched into my Cassandra party looking suspiciously innocent and polite. When I greeted them they had—or most of them had—that faint expression of infant charm and sweetness and light that usually ends with all of us stamping on the table bawling Sweet Adeline, Frankie and Johnnie and arguing that if there are any coppers around here, ask 'em up and we'll tell them exactly what to do.

There were hula-hula girls to arouse our most gallant instincts. A vast cake built by confectioners who must have been brought up in a community of giants, with appetites to match. American turkey— damn these Yanks, they seem to be everywhere. York ham—that's better, me lads. Spring chicken. Sirloin of beef. Fresh lobster—I particularly liked the chap who wanted the casing instead of the innards. Mixed pickles, smoked salmon. Black pearly caviare— damn these Russians, they seem to be everywhere. Anchovy eggs. Sausage rolls. Sardine fingers. And a very Merry Christmas to you all.

The crew of Her Majesty's Ship *Cassandra*, your Cassandra, MY Cassandra, is in excellent good heart.

As the proceedings rose to their defiant and jubilant climax I managed to say a few words to the ship's company. I record with exhausted pleasure that the mightiest roar of the whole thunderous evening broke all records when I proposed the toast of the wives, the sweethearts, the mums, the dads and the nippers at home.

Just off the Equator, and very far from the snowline, I wish all of you who have heard the name of Cassandra, whether it has to do with ships, sealing wax, cabbages, kings, or my particular daily trouble in the public prints, a very happy and a most joyful Christmas.'

Connor finally managed to extricate himself from the alcoholic merryground of endless wardroom parties and flew home via New York and Barbados, where he stayed for a few short days with Hugh Cudlipp who was finishing a book.

After the intense assault-course of international travel in 1961, Connor had a fairly quiet 1962. He went to Paris to see the re-trial of General Salan. It was for this piece of reporting that he was awarded, in the following year, the title of Descriptive Writer of the Year in the first of the Hannen Swaffer Awards.

In 1962 he also journeyed to Rome to observe the Vatican Council called by Pope John; and to the United States—yet again—to interview Dean Acheson, President Kennedy's Secretary of State.

Bill Connor had the travel bug to a much greater extent than most men, and it became far more intense in the last years of his life. So it was hardly surprising when he announced to his family in January 1963 that he was off to America again. This time it was to interview and talk to a large number of people and write a series of articles on what America—and the Americans—thought of Britain. It was a particularly apt time to do this, since President Kennedy and Harold Macmillan had established a new link and understanding between the two countries. Through Kennedy's influence the vast majority of Americans were more favourably inclined towards Britain than they had been for many years, and this showed itself in Connor's reports.

In June 1963 Pope John died. He had been Pope for four all-too-short years. In that time his achievements—and the effects they had throughout the world, and not only in the Catholic Church—were incalculable. Connor wrote of him as 'a kind, good, warm avuncular man. A jolly man. A genial, tubby man. A man without cant or pride . . . . An overwhelmingly lovable man.' Pope John was one of those men of God who found their true expression in practical humanity, not high-minded idealism, and Connor, as always with men like this, respected him. In the sad-yet-triumphant piece that Connor wrote about this good man, he recounted the story of how, when Pope John first became Pope, he still felt as if he were a Cardinal and when he was asked to deal with some matter, said: 'I'll speak to the Pope about that.' But then, realizing and correcting his error, he said: 'But I *am* the Pope. I'll have to take it up with God.' Connor's article was headed: 'He put his arm round the heart of the world.' A good title.

But 1963 had not yet finished. And its appetite for honest and good public men was not yet satisfied, for in November President Kennedy was assassinated in Dallas. On that horrific day the world truly did stand still. Connor flew once more to Washington, shortly after the President's funeral. He visited the old Ford's Theatre in the heart of Washington, the scene of another earlier Presidential assassination, that of Abraham Lincoln. He was deeply saddened to report that the taxi-driver who took him there did not know the way and had to be directed by Connor himself. 'Thus do fame and tragedy fade—at least in the minds of Washington taxi-drivers,' he wrote. He went on to visit the headquarters of the F.B.I., not far from the White House. Here he was shown round by a guide and at the conclusion was given a demonstration of how deadly a machine-gun can be, even if the target is only a paper cut-out at twenty-five yards. He was given the riddled target as a souvenir. 'Guns again. Guns . . .' was his acrimonious comment. Finally he visited Kennedy's grave in Arlington Cemetery. Around it were four Guards of Honour, tall and silent. And armed.

Although he was not to know it at the time, the next year—1964—was to be the last in which he continued his travels at the rate at which he had been going. It was also one of his busiest years. He was out of the country for eight months and he also managed yet another complete round-the-world journey. It started in January with another visit to Israel. The occasion was the visit of the Pope to the Holy Land, one of the first acts of the new Pope Paul, and also the first time that the Head of the Catholic Church had made the pilgrimage.

In mid-February he set out again for Dallas to cover the trial of Jack Ruby, the man who shot President Kennedy's assassin. It was the final squalid little act of the great tragedy; rather like picking up a handful of earth to scatter on the grave, only to discover one had picked up a worm as well. This token expiation for the great collective American sin was almost meaningless. As with the later assassinations of President Kennedy's brother, Robert, and that of Martin Luther King, the American people at large simply put an emotional Elastoplast over the gaping wound, and forgot that it ever happened. Their conscience was salved.

Connor returned from America—and then left again, this time for another trial, that of a number of ex-Nazis who had finally been brought to justice. It was, for Connor, the full turn of the wheel. Twenty-eight years before he had watched the menace of Nazism struggle out of the cradle. Twenty-five years before he had used his pen as a thorn in the side of a British Government apparently unwilling to believe that wars kill people. Eighteen years before he had written about a world trying to patch itself up after the ravages of six years of war against the Nazis and their allies. Three years previously he had observed the fingers of the law closing round the neck of Eichmann. Then, in a courtroom in Frankfurt, the final round-up, the last swabbing up of the blood of so many millions of people, took place. As with the Ruby trial in Dallas, it was more a token than anything else; an action designed so that someone might stand up and say: 'Look, there are no more Nazis. The world is clean again.'

In April, Bill Connor started out on his last round-the-world trip. He went first to Australia, a country that he had not visited since just after the war. It was also the first trip for a very long time that he had made with no specific purpose in mind; he had no particular people to see, or places to visit. It was, in fact, a sort of holiday for Connor, provided by the *Mirror*. His colleagues had become rather alarmed at the pace he was setting himself and were trying to get him to slow down a little. Because of the relaxed nature of his visit he was able to see Australia in a much more leisurely and enjoyable way. In his own words, he found the Australians 'guilty of being friendly, forthright and thirsty'. While he was there he saw 'a kookaburra, which, if you don't know, is an Australian bird of friendly disposition, trod on a quince, sailed in a motor-boat, made friends with a cat named Golly, stood in the shade of a eucalyptus tree, had a couple of schooners of the local beer, watched the surf-riders coming in on the Pacific breakers, got sunburned and learned to say "Goodon-yermate", which is Australian for, "That's fine, chum."' He was also, in a bar near Perth, asked by a total stranger if he would care for a fight. Taken aback by this question, he enquired why. The stranger replied that he thought all Pommies enjoyed a good fight and he merely wanted to make Connor feel at home. This kind of friendliness, though a trifle bizarre, merely added to Connor's impression of the Australians as being 'guilty of open-ness, of warmth, of cordiality and kindness, and I sentence them to live happy ever after in this remarkable and gigantic land'.

While he was in Australia Connor took the opportunity to fulfil a childhood dream. He had, he wrote, been brought up on a dict of books like *Coral Island, Treasure Island, Blue Lagoon* and *Robinson Crusoe*. He went on:

> I heard the surf breaking on the coral reef. I shinned up the waving palm and took the coconuts. I was a personal friend of Long John Silver. I ate myself sick with the imaginary loaves of the breadfruit tree, and I saw Man Friday's footsteps in the sand. I could talk about atolls and cays and in my dreams I steered by the Southern Cross . . .

The dream that came true for him was a visit to the Great Barrier Reef, off the coast of Northern Queensland. He was stunned by the incredible beauty of it all, and by the fact that it was just as he had dreamed it would be. 'It is so like the pre-conceived idea that when it turns out to be exactly true, you could almost laugh.'

From Australia Connor flew to Canada where he had arranged

to meet his wife. Together they took a highly enjoyable holiday, travelling the whole breadth of that vast country. While they were in British Columbia they came upon another piece of uncommon friendliness. This time it was from a friend of Connor's who owned—amongst many other things—an oil well. This is how Connor described the incident:

I know a man who owns an oil well . . . and if you think I'm swanking, you're dead right.

This gentleman said to me: 'I have an oil well. I should be happy to set fire to it for your relaxation should you so desire it.'

The old incendiary in me blazed up at this and I said that nothing would enchant me more. I felt sure that a blazing oil well and I would get on like a house on fire.

We went to the middle of a field out of which emerged a pipe-line, some tanks and a wheel-valve. In the middle of the field was what appeared to be a very large bomb crater.

Someone turned the valve and then with a roar that was louder than a quartet of jet engines, the well caught fire and a cauldron of yellow and orange flame higher than a five-storey house sprang to life. It thundered and it billowed. A pall of black smoke almost blotted the sun out. The heat made you turn your face away from the writhing, wreathing flames.

In fact, so successful was the demonstration that the next field caught fire—which was not the idea at all. The technician who had started the magnificent blaze hastily reversed the process and started beating out the grass and bushes that were by now well alight.

As I said, these Commonwealth chaps really do set themselves out to please.

Connor and his wife returned home after a quick trip over the border into the United States, where they were given a guided tour around an Atlas missile site, and also presented with a stuffed moose-head by a friend with a misplaced sense of humour.

1964 was, of course, another of those years when the American political scene goes raucously beserk. It was the year of the presidential elections. So Connor found himself—for the third time in the year—back in the United States. In July he went to San Francisco to see Senator Barry Goldwater given the Republican Party nomination. He found Goldwater's policies more than a little terrifying, as did, in the final event, the vast majority of the American electorate. (An interesting side note to this was that in fact President Johnson, after election, appeared to carry out Goldwater's ideas almost to the very letter. But then he was the President.)

Connor was back again in November to see Johnson duly elected.

In the interim, however, he had written a book—his fourth and last. It was a short profile of George Brown, a man for whom he had a great deal of admiration, and a man who is, in many ways, surprisingly similar in character. Connor had met Brown for the first time some ten years before. This is how he described the occasion:

It was at some social function. I had no idea that he was George Brown and I am certain that he did not know who I was. Brown, a chubby figure, was standing by the fire-place, telling some political anecdote that I found rather tedious. But he hammered away at it and I grew fascinated at the way he hacked his way through the narrative.

If the tale lacked interest, the method of delivery did not. The sledge-hammer kept hitting the nut. With expressive gestures, with dark luminous eyes, with highly articulate clarity he pursued the gossamer theme.

I was not bored. I was entranced.

I am no recounter of tales and people soon get that glazed look as I develop my dreary theme. The problem is whether to give up as the chill wind of disinterest blows even cooler. The wretched point of your prosaic story is in sight and, if you are as inept as I am, you fear to make it as you stumble onwards. . . .

Not so George Alfred Brown on this particular occasion. As the resistance of the audience increased, the raconteur's attack fiercened.

I said to George Brown (you can talk to him like this if you have a bit of neck like I have): 'If you haven't got all the audience in this room riveted to the spot, you've certainly got me. I admire your tenacity. You must have some of the doggedness of Scott of the Antarctic, of Stanley in pursuit of Livingstone, or of Captain Cook himself. You and I seem to be on a long journey together. Will it be long before land comes in sight?'

'Brother', said George with a grin, 'there's plenty more where this came from. The first hour is the worst. Now to resume . . .'

Connor's book (there is a companion volume written on Harold Wilson by Michael Foot) was published in October at about the time of the General Election which saw the Labour Party returned to power for the first time in thirteen years. It is not a great weighty biography; rather a few thousand very personal words written by Bill Connor about a man he liked.

1965 was distinguished by one thing, and one thing alone. It was the year in which Bill Connor's health started to fail. For a number of years he had not been taking enough care with his diabetes. He had not stuck to the rigid diet that had been laid down for him; he still found that he met his friends on old familiar grounds—pubs. As a result he had been having black-outs. In his own home. In the office. On the train going to or from work. He had shrugged them off, perhaps foolishly, perhaps out of sheer bloody-mindedness, saying, 'Don't worry. I'm all right. Stop bothering me.' One week-end he and his brother Mick, together with his old friend Len Wise, decided to go to their favourite inn for a quiet drink before going on to see someone. While he was in the pub, standing talking in his hunched-shouldered way, Connor had another black-out. Only this time it was serious. He was a heavy man, weighing some fifteen-odd stone, and as he fell he hit his head on the edge of a chair-back. The result was a fractured skull. He was admitted to High Wycombe Memorial Hospital, where he spent four or five weeks.

But even this could not keep him from his typewriter. He wrote an article for the *New Statesman* about his experience. It was a sad, poignant and highly moving article. He called it 'The Going of Him'.

It was absurdly like arriving at a party very late and knowing that it was all over and that everyone who had any sense would be in bed. They were, and the place was almost in total darkness.

Mind you, they made me very welcome.

The public ward (Surgical) of a hospital just before midnight is not the gayest of places but I had valid admission tickets: a fractured skull; blood from the left ear (a very good credential); a high temperature; accelerated respiration; post-shock shivers; and, almost certainly, concussion.

Peter Sellers was, of course, the late-duty-house-doctor-receptionist and was brimming over with the dusky charm and real concern of his kind that sometimes contrasts sharply with the brusque impartiality of the paler brethren who, occasionally, I have found, are inclined to regard illness or accident as a matter of guilt on the part of the patient.

How did it happen? asked Mr Sellers. What a shame. Where did it happen? What a pity. No, don't worry about the blood on the pillow. Just relax. We'll take care of you. All will be well.

My heart did not go pit-a-pat but my head went honkety-tonk all right. Then on to the rubber-tyred trolley and head foremost towards the ward.

Nurses waiting and the Night Sister in the background. Again the polished charm, the practised efficiency, the enfolding silence and the comforting dark.

I roll on to one of those absurdly high beds that later I am told is not so darned silly as you might think. Making beds is back-breaking work, especially with people lying in them. The lower the beds are, the more spine-twisting they are for the people who have to make them. Can I have another pillow? No. Head injuries should lie flat in bed. May I have a sleeping tablet? No. Not allowed in cases like yours.

I have never felt more alert, more detached, more clinically observant. Maybe that clout on the head is doing things for me. I feel I can step outside myself and just watch; watch, with interest, watch with amusement, watch with pleasing self-disdain.

There are twenty-five beds in the ward. On the left three prostates (you soon learn to separate the maladies from their owners in hospital), are breathing heavily and a fourth, a motor-cycle mix-up suspended in the inevitable rigging, is gently snoring.

I learned later that the prostates were 'done' early that morning and were making swift recoveries from this once fearsome operation.

On my right was an old man in his eighties called Harry, who was sleeping peacefully. He later introduced himself to me in a gruff, friendly voice with a splendid touch of old-fashioned formality: 'Neighbour on my left!' he shouted. 'My name is Harry. What's yours?'

'Bill,' says I.

I tried to get to sleep but the mental light inside me glowed maddeningly brighter. You know you can't sleep. You know exactly why. Within seven paces of the foot of your bed there is a man dying.

An old, old man—nearly eighty-five years of age as it turned out—is coming to the end of the road. This is the last big sleep. He was hit by a car five days ago and has not recovered consciousness.

The mind, already buried, is dead in the tomb of the failing body. With him, night after night, has been his son. A burly impassive figure keeping the last pointless but brave vigil. He stands almost motionless and rarely sits down.

The curtains are drawn round the dying man but there is a wide gap left open. Above his head is a light covered with a red duster. He rests on the high pillows and his face, flushed and sharp, has an angry look.

I am told by people who know about these things that the last expression on people's faces, especially those killed in accidents, is often one of surprised indignation.

They wear the why-should-this-happen-to-me look.

The dying man breathes fiercely, harshly and at double the normal speed. So regular and so noisy is his respiration that you get the impression that he must be in some mechanical iron lung.

One ... two ... one-two-one-two like stamping feet on a parade ground. In-out-in-out-in-out, chest heaving. The minutes crawl by to the accompaniment of this terrible rhythm.

The lone relative—the shadow against the curtain—looks on. The old life that began in the 1880s is gasping its way to the last rendezvous.

Disraeli had just died when he was born and his mother first looked on her little male child. Gladstone had nearly twenty years to live. Stage coaches were running regularly in the Lake District and between London and Brighton and London and Oxford.

Tallow candles were a penny a dozen and Robert Louis Stevenson was describing electric light as fit only for the corridors of lunatic asylums.

Hiram Maxim was hard at work on his machine-gun and John Henry Newman had written Lead Kindly Light.

This was the surrounding dawn of the beginning of the life of the aged man so near to me. He was in his late teens the night Mafeking was relieved.

He was a fully grown man when the guns in France could be heard in London in the summer of 1914. He was just sixty when the Second World War sent 30,000,000 people to their graves before their time.

When he was born there was no motor-car, no flying machine, no radio, no television, and during his eight decades man increased his travelling speed from eighty miles an hour in an express train to 18,000 miles an hour encircling the globe in eighty minutes.

Now the tumultuous years were ending.

As the pale water-colour wash of dawn lightened the east windows of the ward the stertorous breathing suddenly stopped.

Silence.

You felt the whole ward was awake, roused by the ticking of the clock that had abruptly ceased.

The Sister was at his side within seconds. The nurses, with ballet precision, tallest on the left, shortest on the right, stood outside the curtain looking in. The soundless scene was frozen.

The breathing cut in again as suddenly as it had cut out. They held his pulse, moved silently away from the bed and resumed their seats at the table.

Three minutes later the tearing, wheezing sound stopped again. Had the old heart really failed this time? In a trice the oxygen cylinder on its rubber-tyred cradle was wheeled in. A faint hiss.

Some thirty people were listening. Not a sound. The mind cried out for a whimper, for a prayer, even for the tolling of a bell. Anything but this aching nothing.

A nurse switched on her torch and the thin searching beam flickered up the wall to the ward clock. A professional touch to read the time of death—4.33 a.m.

Still the freezing quiet.

Then from the bed next to me, Harry spoke—a gruff, whiskery voice that said hoarsely but loudly: 'Gorn!' There was no emotion. Just a dispassionate observation.

Harry, with terrifying matter-of-factness, was simply recording the fact that the old man had gone.

It so happens that recently I attended the exultant and splendid service of Sir Winston Churchill at St Paul's, perhaps the most triumphant farewell in the history of mankind, with flags flaunting, trumpets sounding and a great congregation singing defiance of death—not lamentation.

Here in this hospital ward was the obverse side of the coin of death inscribed with surely the tersest of all epitaphs—'Gorn!'

Depending on how you think about these things, a life was snuffed out for ever, a soul was winging its way to Paradise, a spirit was adrift on the River Lethe.

The faithful son, the silent Absalom, gathered up a few of his father's pieces and disappeared.

With a strange little secular ceremony they pulled all the curtains around our cubicles when they wheeled the old fellow away. Soon they washed us. They fed us.

The paper boy came in and Harry greeted the new-born day with a rousing description of the Soccer virtues of West Ham and the motor-cycle smash-up case chattered with endless cheerful idiocy about Sandown Park.

I think they know how to do these sombre things in the public wards. Arm in arm, dispassion and compassion go rather well.

Looking back, one realizes that this article was a very vital one for Connor. If he ever had one fear about his writing it was that it might suddenly dry up. His accident certainly must have worried him on this point. 'The Going of Him' was the acid test, and one which he must have felt he had passed.

By July he was out of hospital and well enough to go on a recuperative holiday. He and his wife and younger son went to the Greek Islands for three weeks. They came back relaxed and tanned. Connor was raring to go again. But even at this early stage it is probable that he knew that he was breaking up physically. For the first time in his life he tried very hard to do exactly as the doctors had told him.

One immediate after-effect of his accident distressed him greatly. His hearing in one ear had been affected; he was very deaf. For much of his life he had been a listener; he obtained a lot of his material from letting other people talk and listening to conversation. Now it became an effort for him. Instead of being able to sit and let the voices wash over him, he had to concentrate. It infuriated him to have to ask people to speak up. It made him very testy. For a brief period he even tried a hearing aid, but then lost his patience with it and threw it away. Deafness has a cruel effect on people's personalities; it makes them withdrawn. With Bill Connor—who was already an introvert—it became very noticeable. He began to feel like an outsider and, behaving like one, he drew his shell ever closer around himself.

On 30 November 1965, Bill Connor had a letter from 10 Downing Street. It read:

Sir,

I am asked by the Prime Minister to inform you, in strictest confidence, that he has it in mind, on the occasion of the forthcoming list of New Year Honours, to submit your name to the Queen with a recommendation that Her Majesty may be graciously pleased to approve that the Honour of Knighthood be conferred upon you. . . .

Connor was flabbergasted. It was something that he had never—even in the wildest of moments—have dreamed of. There had been no inkling, no indication that anything of this sort had been in the wind. For nearly three weeks he went around wondering whether he should accept. He told no one—not even his wife or family. Then, one Sunday shortly before Christmas, he invited Hugh Cudlipp and his wife over to lunch. It was a pleasant convivial meal, with the usual kind of light chatter between friends. After the meal was over and cleared away he said: 'By the way, I've got something to show you.' He disappeared to his study for a moment and came back with the letter. He handed it to his wife, who read it and passed it on without a word. Every single person in the room read it in silence, without comment. 'Do you think I should accept?' he asked, when no one spoke. Their answer was, naturally enough, yes.

He attended an Investiture at Buckingham Palace on 15 February 1966 where he was knighted by Queen Elizabeth, The Queen Mother. Afterwards he held a small luncheon party for his family and friends.

Bill Connor—Cassandra—was now Sir William. And the whole of Fleet Street was cock-a-hoop about it. Though the newspaper business had had other knights in their midst before, this was the first time that one of them had been given the accolade for services to journalism. They regarded it as a just reward for a very distinguished career, and they bathed in the reflected glory. It had long been felt by the inhabitants of Fleet Street that the Fourth Estate had been ignored and neglected in the Honours Lists. Now that wrong had been righted, and in a way that gained universal approval.

Connor had his leg pulled mercilessly—especially since some years before he had written a *Daily Mirror* Spotlight on Honours

Kc

and Awards pamphlet that had been pretty scathing. He enjoyed the joke enormously. And as a morale booster it worked wonders. For a while he was his old volatile, ebullient self again. He was back in harness, writing his column, and enjoying it a great deal.

Then, at the beginning of March, the second and more serious blow to his health came. He was rushed back to High Wycombe Hospital with a massive stomach haemorrhage. For four days he appeared to be dying. The doctors were giving him almost constant blood transfusions to try to build up his strength for a vital operation. They succeeded, when all appeared lost. The operation was carried out, and he stood it well. The news was rushed to his friends in the *Mirror*. Bill Herbert hurried into Hugh Cudlipp's room, and said with a triumphant cry: 'He's pulled through! The old bugger's done it again.' The sentiment was deeply heartfelt, even if the language was less than couth.

Slowly Connor climbed back up the ladder of recuperation. But he had another problem to deal with besides the deafness. His internal clock—that strange body mechanism that always takes a beating when one goes on a long aeroplane flight—had, in his own words, 'slipped six hours'. He found great difficulty in sleeping and, for that matter, staying awake. He would go to bed at ten or eleven at night and not get to sleep until four or five in the morning. Then he would be desperately tired and dozy until about two o'clock in the afternoon. Sleeping pills were useless; they merely left him comatose for long periods of the day or night. Then, accidently, he found a strange and unlikely solution to his problem. He flew to the United States—for the last time—to do some research for a series of articles he was writing on the problem of drug addiction. He found, for the first time, and to his great astonishment and delight, that the six hours time difference between America and Great Britain did not affect him at all. In fact, when he arrived he found that his own time-clock coincided perfectly with Eastern Standard Time. But this of course was only a temporary relief. When he returned things were just as bad. His health was really beginning to crumble.

In September 1966 he flew to Berlin to watch the release of the Nazi war criminals von Schirach and Speer from Spandau prison. Only Hess was left. Connor wrote that perhaps it was time to show some mercy to this shambling hulk of a man, evil though he might be.

In October Connor went to Canada to take a look at the preparations being made for Expo '67. He also visited some paper pulp mills owned by the *Mirror* and wrote a piece commenting on how many trees were used every day so that his column might appear.

But the spark was dying. From time to time a breath of air would make it glow brighter, but then afterwards it would always be duller. Bill Connor knew he was a dying man. He accepted it as calmly as possible, told no one until he was certain—and even then, only one person—and went about the business of tidying up his affairs.

In February 1967—after spending a quiet and sombre Christmas with his family—he was admitted to King Edward VII Hospital in London for sedation treatment for his insomnia. He was there for three weeks, and then returned home. While he was at home again he collapsed for the last time. An ambulance rushed him to High Wycombe. He was having terrible haemorrhages. After ten days spent there he was moved to St Bartholomews Hospital in London. A fortnight later, on 6 April, he died. He would have been fifty-eight years old had he lived three weeks longer.

CHAPTER NINE

UNDER THE SPOTLIGHT

T HE state of celebrity is a paradoxical one. In attaining it, a person must face a certain amount of publicity. The name must appear in print, the face has to be seen in prominent company. If a television appearance can be organized, so much the better. A plethora of personal details usually accompanies the operation. The public—insatiable animal that it is—demands to know more and more. Age, height and colour of eyes is not enough. In becoming a celebrity, a person is adopted by a large number of people as their property. In extreme cases the adoption is accompanied by a fervour bordering on hysteria. Ask any Beatles' fan. A celebrity must be willing to be put under the spotlight, all the better to see him with. But the strange thing is that having undergone this treatment, this public exposure and this intimate scrutiny, the first question anyone asks of a famous man—or woman—is: 'Yes, but what's he [or she] *really* like?'

'What was he *really* like?' A simple question, and one which is the true reason for any biography. A simple question—just five words. Yet always the most difficult for anyone to answer. Any one person asked that question usually has a definite answer. But two people can have conflicting answers. Far better, then, to play the jurist; present the evidence and let the questioner make up his own mind.

What was Bill Connor *really* like? A simple answer is that he was a complex, fascinating man. But then that is not really an answer at all. Like 'We'll tell you when you're older' or 'It's difficult—you probably wouldn't understand'; an answer that invites more curiosity and a desire to know more. So we must subdivide the question a little further and we end up with two questions. 'What was Bill Connor, journalist, "Cassandra" of the *Daily Mirror*, really like?' and 'What was Bill Connor, the man, really like?'

Physically, he was a big man. At least he was after the war. Before he went into the army he had been very, very slim, with a thin face, big round glasses and hair parted in the middle. But soon after he went into the Army he began to put on a lot of weight—weight that he never lost. He had very blue eyes and a habit of looking over the top of his spectacles. He was an inch under six feet, though he always looked shorter, partly as a result of his build and partly because he always stood slightly slumped. He had big hands, with shortish spatulate fingers—strong, capable hands, not in the least bit the hands of an aesthete. His voice was quiet and, rather surprisingly, higher than one would have suspected from his appearance. He always wore a slightly lugubrious expression; sombre, with more than a hint of tired sadness about it. When talking—or, as he preferred, listening —to someone, he would watch him keenly over the top of his glasses, with a direct unblinking gaze. He always dressed rather quietly—white shirt, simple patterned tie and restrained suit, usually grey. Clothes never interested him; they were merely something to wear. In fact, his lack of interest in the clothes he wore once produced an amusing incident. He went to his tailor to order a new suit—'the same as the last one you made for me'. His tailor, surveying the ever-so-slightly fraying cuffs and the baggy trousers said, very deferentially: 'Perhaps we could take the trousers in a bit, sir. If I may be so bold, sir, they do make us look a little like Mr Kruschev.'

Next, the professional face, the mask presented to the public, to his readers. He was, or would have been called so in Elizabethan times, a 'choleric' man. Irascible, excitable, passionate, testy and tetchy. A man who dealt in verbal broadsides rather than the quiet, hidden snipe. He used his pen like a club rather than a switch. The sandbag method was the one he favoured. If you were a fan you loved it. Nouns would fly out of the barrels and come thumping over. Adverbs would follow. Adjectives would be used like grapeshot, peppering their target. Verbs, participles and all the other grammatical armaments were used to great effect. The chosen target would slowly sink beneath the waves, like some clumsy, dismasted wooden warship. But if you were not a fan, then the picture was quite different. Here was a nasty, roaring Juggernaut, who belaboured everything and everyone in a most violent manner. To the non-fans he could be like the

school bully, who abuses his power to frighten lesser beings. He
was bigger than them—and they could not fight back. A newspaper is a mighty powerful thing. Anyone who works in one is
in a lofty and tactically superior position. Looking down, he can
see all below, and strike, if that is in his nature. But, of course,
there were more people, among his readers, who liked than
disliked him. Those who felt strongly about him, simply stopped
reading him.

Then there was another—and apparently contradictory—
side to Bill Connor, journalist. He had warmth. He could write
a column that would make the reader feel snug and cosy. After all,
he headed his piece on Pope John: 'He put his arm round the
heart of the world.' Bill Connor could do that, not with the
world, but with his readers. He could write—and often did—of
the things that made them feel at home, of the toys of their
childhood, the names of long-forgotten cars or trams, or street
markets that had been buried under concrete to make room for
supermarkets. The arrow of nostalgia was one that was often
taken from his quiver and loosed with unerring accuracy. After
the memorial service held for him in St Paul's on 21 April 1967,
Marjorie Proops, the *Mirror*'s brilliant woman writer, was leaving
quietly by a side door. As she slipped away she was stopped by an
old lady with a very tear-stained face who said to her: 'Don't you
go too, Miss Proops. You're the only one left who writes for us
people, now that he's gone.' A touching epitaph—and one that
sums up the regard and affection that many of his readers felt for
him. They could identify themselves with him. He spoke their
language, understood their fears and problems, was their
champion.

What else then? What other sides were there to his writing?
There was the humour. Connor could make you laugh. Not just
smile or giggle. Laugh—great belly-shaking guffaws. And the
funny columns were the ones that he gave him the most pleasure.
If he wrote a serious one, no matter how good, he rarely bothered
to ask for your comments. But when he'd produced an amusing
column he'd very often say, 'Well, how did you like it?' A sense of
humour was very important to him, and a necessary qualification
in anyone who was to be a friend.

Humour in his writing took a number of forms. He was an inveterate collector of awful puns which he would retail in his column. He was so partial to them, and they appeared with such regularity, that he indulged in a little flight of fantasy about them. He invented a mythical Joke Factory, which he sited somewhere in Penge, where little wizened men sweated all day long constructing excruciating puns. He claimed that the best were 'carved from solid oak' and that to be really good, they had to be really bad. He had a small circle of friends who would contribute to the pile from time to time. And readers joined in the fun and sent him in a constant stream of terrible jokes. He adored them all. For instance here is one that appeared—or rather escaped—in February 1962.

Red-eyed am I this morning. And if you think that is a disgraceful style of sentence, you are dead right. But then you haven't been up all night working at The Joke Factory, Penge, S.E.20. There is something about Penge that seems to suit a Joke Factory specializing in hideous puns.

Last night we managed to build a real stinker.

It is a particularly offensive specimen, but it has the essential character of being laboriously contrived. You can see the rotten laths in the plaster. Stand by. We're off.

There is a drink called a Daiquiri—pronounced 'Dackery'. It is made with rum, lemon squash and angostura bitters and is very popular in the United States.

A certain doctor in Savannah (note the geographical touch that has absolutely nothing to do with the story) always used to frequent the same bar where he always had the same drink: a Daiquiri served with a peanut in it.

One day the barman had run out of peanuts and put a hickory nut instead into the drink.

'Hey, barkeep,' said the doctor, 'there's something different about this Daiquiri.'

Said the barkeep: 'Sure is. That's a Hickory, Daiquiri, Doc.'

And just in case you're still on your feet, though groggy, here's another from the Cassandra Collection.

Forward into the abyss of unspeakable puns! Look at the ghastly clockwork of this one. It cannot be true, but how I love to linger over the toiling creaking care of the man who made it up. He went through with it to the bitter end. Here goes:

A nephew of Mr Syngman Rhee—the old gentleman of Korea—emigrated to the United States and got himself a job on *Life* magazine. He went on a mighty spree one day in New York and vanished. *Life*, worried about the welfare of their interesting employee, sent out a search party and sure enough the stray lamb was found dazed but happy in one of the innumerable taverns that used to make Third Avenue the finest street in Manhattan.

The chief rescuer gave a great cry of triumph and shouted: 'Ah, sweet Mr Rhee of Life! At last I've found you!'

Bill Connor was often terribly funny in his ordinary descriptive writing. He would take a perfectly ordinary thing and, simply by juggling and balancing words, could have one giggling helplessly over the breakfast table. Here are a few examples.

On his self-confessed, inimitable and awful piano rendering of 'Nellie Dean':

The atmosphere is unbearably tense and there is a wave of primeval fear and fascination as I make the first tremendous assault. It is a musical Battle of the Bulge. I am Marshal Ludwig Beethoven Montgomery. I am Marshal Johann Sebastian Rundstedt.

The force and the incredible violence with which I hit the wrong notes, get the tempo all snarled up and massacre the melody with my bare hands is like Myra Hess, Rubinstein and Artur Schnabel in reverse. Medical specialists say that it is one of the most punishing experiences known to the human ear. . . .

I shall always remember one of the finest tributes ever given to me after I had finished with 'Nellie Dean'. It came from a foundry worker who used to be a riveter and knew something about the harsher sounds of life.

He was trembling slightly as he gripped my hand and he murmured: 'Unforgettable . . . and absolutely unforgivable.'

On a hangover:

Bright lights hurt the eyes, and jeering gibbering people from the night before seem to whisper in your ears, and then fade with horrible mocking laughter into silence.

The finger nails are brittle, and your skin hangs on you like an old second-hand suit.

Your feet appear to be swollen, and walking is like wading through a swamp of lumpy thick custard. . . .

When you brush your hair you are certain that there is no top to your skull, and your brain stands naked and throbbing in the stabbing air. . . .

You have no sense of touch and your fingertips feel with all the acuteness of decayed firewood smeared with putty. . . .

You want to sleep, but when you close your eyes you are dizzy, and you heel over like a waterlogged barrel crammed with old sodden cabbage stalks in the Grand Junction Canal. . . .

On gout:

It is curious the things that make people happy, for whenever I mention to people that I have had gout, their faces light up and they guffaw with glee.

I ask them if they ever had toothache in the foot. They hold their sides shrieking with joy.

I explain that gout is like walking on your eyeballs. The tears run down their cheeks.

I describe the crushing, terrifying weight of but a single sheet upon the tortured foot. They cry with ecstasy. . . .

On the taste of turkey:

What a shocking fraud the turkey is.

In life, preposterous, insulting—that foolish noise they make to scare you away! In death—unpalatable. The turkey has practically no taste except a dry fibrous flavour reminiscent of a mixture of warmed up plaster of paris and horsehair. The texture is like wet sawdust and the whole vast feathered swindle has the piquancy of a boiled mattress. . . .

On the terminology of estate agents' advertisements:

You need a glossary to understand the lingo. 'Easily maintained' means it badly needs propping up. 'Superbly restored with no expense spared' means that the price is so outrageously high that even the vendors dare not mention it. 'Miniature' means no room to swing a cat. 'Within thirty-five minutes of Waterloo' means eighty miles to the south-east of London flying by specially-chartered helicopter. 'Charming' means revolting. 'Picturesque' means the same as charming—only held together with poison ivy. 'Delightful' means disgusting. 'Compact' means suitable for dwarfs. 'Home of the future' means unsold in the present and likely to remain so. 'Adjoining green belt' means Slough. 'Immaculate' means badly needs a lick of paint. 'Antique oak-beamed' means new black-painted pine. 'Manageable garden' means gnarled nasturtiums with room to swing a dead rat on a short string. 'Important' means pretentious. 'Imposing' means menacing. 'Secluded' means set in a swamp in the middle of a forest. 'Spacious' means anything from ten to twenty damp bedrooms with a coal-fired boiler that was originally designed by Brunel for his monstrous ship the *Great Eastern*. And 'enchanting surroundings with modern conveniences' means there's a pylon at the bottom of the garden. . . .

Connor's writing was always personal. He used his column to state his own beliefs, forcefully and usually irrevocably. But there were the odd occasions when he did change his mind as a result of events subsequent to writing a piece. This was after he had written about a person and had then met him or discovered more about him. On those few occasions when he did change his mind publicly he could be generous in righting the situation. For instance in 1954 he wrote this of Billy Graham, who was making his first crusade to this country:

> William Graham is the smartest, the smoothest, the slickest and the most graceful opponent of iniquity I have ever seen in my life.

Connor went on to describe him as 'this Hollywood version of John the Baptist'. But he was completely disarmed by Billy Graham who wrote to him suggesting they meet. A suitably appropriate venue was chosen—a pub named The Baptist's Head. The meeting was a huge success. Connor took to Billy Graham instantly, and was won over by his manner. He had expected a Bible-thumping fanatic; he found instead 'a good man . . . a simple man . . . and goodness and simplicity are a couple of tough customers'. Having met and come to like Graham, Bill Connor wrote an article saying so. He explained in detail how his opinion had been changed and finished up by saying: 'I never thought that friendliness had such a sharp cutting edge. I never thought simplicity could cudgel us sinners so damned hard. We live and learn.'

Another instance of Connor's having to revise an opinion concerned Gilbert Harding. They had met in a restaurant—and had a furious row, one that was spoken of in awed tones by those who had been present to witness it. A year later, in 1954, Connor arranged an interview with him (it was for the series of profiles on famous people he was doing at the time). In a letter to Harding arranging a luncheon for the two of them, he wrote a postscript that was typical of him, 'Insults will be worn'. The lunch duly took place. It was a resounding success. Connor wrote his article— a warm, friendly one. He described Gilbert Harding as a 'gruff old teddy bear'. He found him 'ill-tempered and immensely good-humoured. He is fierce and he is timid. He is arrogant and he is surprisingly humble. He is crammed with likes and dislikes and loaded with endless assertions and countless doubts.' The article was entitled 'Old Lonely Heart'.

One way of finding out what a man is like is to ask his fellow workers and contemporaries. Being in the same business they know what it is really like—and they can see the man with his defences down. So let us see what some of his fellow journalists thought of Bill Connor, from their various viewpoints of an office next door, or along the corridor, or just across the road. Cecil King, who was able to observe Connor for the whole of his career at the *Mirror* found him 'a prickly man' but as a writer 'probably the best of his time . . . certainly way in front of any other English writer'. King was also impressed by Connor's courage and sincerity as a journalist.

Sidney Jacobson, now Chairman of Odhams Newspapers who had worked with Connor on *Public Opinion* and had later joined the *Daily Mirror* as Political Editor, admired the professionalism of the column. 'It was always finely polished,' he says. Jacobson was also impressed by the way Connor helped newcomers to the paper. 'When I first arrived at the *Daily Mirror* in 1955, Bill arranged a lunch for me at Simpsons and introduced me to all the people I should know. It was very thoughtful of him.' Jacobson's own preference amongst the varied types of columns was for the off-beat ones, especially those on cooking. He tells the story of how his wife had tried to make a soup from one of Connor's recipes. It was an unmitigated disaster. When Connor was told of this culinary mishap he sent Jacobson's wife a telegram saying simply, 'Soupy life is not as simple as you think.'

Lionel Crane, for a long time one of the *Mirror's* New York correspondents, was another who liked Connor as a professional. He was also fascinated to know what made him tick. He once asked Connor to what he ascribed his success. 'I was brought up in the gutter but my eyes were on the stars,' was Connor's epigrammatic reply. 'He said it with a twinkle in his eyes,' recalls Crane, 'so I didn't know whether he was pulling my leg or not.'

Connor got on well with his editors—with the exception of Sylvester Bolam. His relationships with them were never what one might call tranquil. They had to be turbulent to survive. Perhaps the reason for his never seeing eye to eye with Bolam was that Bolam was a 'dry stick', a man who would not and could not indulge in the kind of boisterous verbal in-fighting that was so much a part of a successful friendship with Connor. For Bartholomew—though never editor—he had enormous respect for Bart taught him more about the newspaper business than any other single man. He had also given him his opportunity right at the start and had been the first to give him the completely free hand that he needed in writing his column. There were others later on who left Connor with that same freedom, but he always was grateful to the man who first liberated him. With Cowley there was a kind of mutual respect. Neither felt very strongly about the other; Connor was too busy trying to establish himself and Cowley was absorbed in trying to keep up with Bartholomew's frantic pace for either of them to get to know one another intimately. They viewed each other with a guarded curiosity. Of the post-war editors without doubt the one who came closest to Connor in rough-and-tumble badinage was Jack Nener. If you became involved in a conversation with the two of them you had to be thick-skinned and quick-witted. You were either quick—or dead. They fought furiously—and joyfully. Each inspired the other to even greater heights of friendly abuse. Nener scored a major victory over Connor when he referred to him once, in Connor's presence, as a 'Pickwick with a heart of lead'. Connor was delighted with this description; it was just the kind of low-level sudden attack insult that he himself was expert in. They had a kind of code between them: when Connor was being just normally insulting he would call Nener either 'Jack' or 'Nener'. But on those occasions when there was true animosity between them, Connor would call him 'Stanley'—a name that Nener disliked. Connor found in Nener a soul mate, someone who spoke his language—no mean achievement—and someone who felt much the same way about things. Theirs was a very stimulating friendship.

Nener says that he found his relationship with Connor a little strange. Connor, according to him, was always a little suspicious of editors, who were invented, so he thought, to try to curb his activities. This was due to the fact that by the time Jack Nener arrived as editor, Connor was one of the elders of the newspaper. The present editor, Lee Howard, who replaced Jack Nener in 1961, also found this to a certain extent. When he first became editor he was a shade wary of how he would be greeted by Connor. But a friendly relationship was very quickly established. From time to time Howard would drop in to Connor's office for a chat. Connor would immediately stop whatever he was doing and talk to Howard. Their conversations might last anything from a minute to an hour. It was only long after many such apparently casual conversations that Howard discovered that Connor had stopped writing his column—usually sacrosanct—to take time to talk to him. Howard found him 'imperturbable'—he would simply get on with the column and catch up again after Howard had left. He didn't complain about it; he just made sure that it was ready in time. Howard found him very easy to work with; he liked the fearless quality of the man, but one thing could occasionally be a little irritating. Connor was in the habit of making out a list of subjects that he was going to write about each day and send it in to the daily editorial conference, held every morning. When the list came in to Howard he very often found that Connor had pinched the best stories of the day, and Howard and the others had to revise their ideas and do something else instead for their leaders.

Tom Tullett is the head of the *Daily Mirror* Crime Bureau. An ex-C.I.D. man himself, he was often able to tip Bill Connor the nod about an apparently innocent episode before it became a big story. In this way Connor was able sometimes to get his story in first. Tom Tullett says of him: 'Bill Connor was a great professional. He liked good reporting and was quick to hand out congratulations. "Good piece that was, my boy," he would say. "How did you get it?" The eyes, over the glasses, always asked for the truth. So when you told him the ins and outs, the details of the operations, he would say triumphantly to the assembled throng in one Fleet Street pub or another: "I'll tell you what. They don't teach you that at the bloody polytechnic." '

Many times when Bill Connor went abroad for a story he took a photographer with him, and always the same one, Bela Zola. There were three reasons for always choosing Zola. First he is a superb photographer; secondly he speaks ten languages; and thirdly Connor liked him immensely. Bela Zola knew and worked with him for some twenty-three years. They first met during the war, in Rome, when Connor was with the Forces newspaper, *Union Jack*. 'At first sight,' Zola remembers, 'he was a rather large captain with a very stern mien. It took me only a few moments to discover that this was nature's protection for one of the kindest and most generous of men.'

Joyce Gillard, who was Connor's secretary for the last three years of his life, also found him kind and thoughtful. She enjoyed working for him. 'There was always laughter in his office— and he always kept the kitty well supplied with tea money.' She says that her job was 'a plum', the one that nearly all the other secretaries vied with her for.

Perhaps the most perspicacious of Bill Connor's obituarists was Donald Zec, brother of the cartoonist, who was also a colleague. Obituaries are, by their very nature, one-sided. They tend to be too effusive, too weighed down with praise and emotion, to be a true picture of a man. But Zec, in the one that he wrote for the *Sunday Times*, captured more than any other

some of the true aspects, the real facets of Bill Connor. No apology
is made for printing it here in full:

> Sir William Connor, 'Cassandra' of the *Daily Mirror,* was loved
> because in this uneasy business of putting words together and making
> them soar if not sing, he was the master.
>
> It is not merely that he composed and orchestrated his columns
> like symphonies—daring you to cough between the movements.
> Nor was it only because of the staggering achievement of producing
> daily columns almost without let-up through thirty turbulent years.
>
> It was the astonishing range of his vision which, like Jodrell Bank,
> picked up the faintest signal that might have been glad to bleep
> unnoticed.
>
> Followers of this gruff genial sage marvelled at his prodigious out-
> put. They should have observed the input. It ranged over all things
> written from the Highway Code to the Holy Bible. Pedigree Vege-
> table Seeds and Homer. Practical Woodwork and the Five Books of
> Moses.
>
> Churchmen who sought to admonish this sinner by hurling care-
> fully selected Bible passages at him were astonished to receive a direct
> hit in the pulpit with equally relevant sections from the scriptures.
>
> Anyway it is not wise to mix it with a man who begins a column:
> 'I know the density of mercury and it is 13·59 gm. per c.c. at zero
> Centigrade.'
>
> Nor with one who can deliver himself of this chilling irony:
> 'Harry Allen, the public hangman and Lancashire publican—strange
> how these two trades involving drops seem to go together—has
> retired after 25 years public service.'
>
> No ordinary journalist is expected to be an instant oracle on jazz,
> steam trains, clocks, roses, soups, vintage cars and the Versailles Treaty.
>
> But if there are others, can they also sing all the verses of 'Frankie
> and Johnnie', play Handel's Largo unaided on a piano, grow gigantic
> sunflowers and write the definitive work on one man and his cats?
>
> Cassandra's imaginary conversations with his stomach were
> hilarious masterpieces. Certainly no other writer can claim that his
> intestines were syndicated around the world.
>
> When he was not castigating a wayward politician, explosively
> condemning some bureaucratic injustice, or dressing down a dressed
> up piano-player, he would idly turn the pages of the telephone book
> and milk some creamy prose out of that too. When in early days, he
> went out on an adjectival rampage, he left Roget tongue-tied at the
> post and the Concise Oxford Dictionary went out to look for words.

And, of course, only a consumate craftsman—the first to win the Hannen Swaffer award as the Descriptive Writer of the Year—could glory in the truly ghastly pun.

He was, as I recall it, the first to put all his 'Basques in one exit'. And like the comment on the de Mille classic, 'loved Ben, hated Hur', he re-issued the gem when the next generation was at the turnstiles.

He was big, he was kindly, he was compassionate and, when the occasion called for it, as cussed as they come.

He did not relish formal gatherings and I trust he would concede that no simpering cocktail party would have been wrecked without him.

He would frown into these gatherings, take up a strong defensive position behind his spectacles and wait for the frontal assault from anyone out in search of an argument. The unhappy victims swiftly discovered what it must be like to be spun into a combine harvester—cut, baled and bounced out into the wilderness.

He suffered fools badly—but the weak, the down-trodden and the underprivileged found Cass at his most kindly and benevolent.

And it helped if you liked cats. He loved them almost obsessively, leading to this defiant, take-on-all-comers first sentence in a column: 'My cat is the finest cat in Bucks south of a line drawn from Ludgershall to Wendover.'

In argument this half-Irish, half-Scottish protagonist was like his writing—forceful, eloquent and sometimes crushing. Roaring into action, one arm swinging out, the back of the hand swaying ahead of the main force was awesome to behold—if you did not sense the chuckle that was germinating inside it all. Racial discrimination, notably the explosive overtones of apartheid in South Africa, produced some of his most passionate denunciations.

He had seen Fascism for what it was long before it detonated Europe—and the written records prove it. Hitler, Goebbels, Ribbentrop, Mussolini before the war, Senator McCarthy after—endured a verbal onslaught unequalled in its intensity, unmatched in its devastating eloquence.

He chronicled brilliantly and incisively almost every major event across the world. The H-bomb test off Christmas Island saddened him. He saw the mushroom cloud as 'like an oil painting from hell'.

And he was saddened, too, by the wretchedness of homeless Italian street urchins; the humiliating struggle of Father Huddleston in South Africa; and the icy composure of Eichmann in that glass booth in Jerusalem.

The knighthood last year, a tribute rejoiced in by the entire pro-
fession, was just as timely. His health was already failing, though
miraculously his columns were immaculate as ever—superbly constructed, brilliantly worked out.

At 11.30 precisely (we do not approximate in the presence of the
master) on a Saturday night, October 8th 1960, a remarkable ceremony took place in a London hotel ballroom. A muster of cheering
sailors lifted his bulky figure upon their shoulders and paraded him
around the room. The occasion—to mark the commission of H.M.S.
Cassandra before she sailed to the Far East.

Clearly the urge to link this irascible craft with my formidable
colleague was irresistible. Here was a pugnacious vessel, a gentle soul
in peaceful waters, but capable of delivering a blistering bombard-
ment when aroused.

'Bon Voyage' acquires an added meaning.

These are all impressions of colleagues and fellow journalists.
Generally, they admired him as a writer. As a person they found
Connor's usually-friendly irascibility stimulating. Engaging in a
verbal battle with him on amicable grounds was part and parcel of
a ritual. If you could meet and match Connor on his own terms
then you were generally accepted by him. It could be tough—
but then journalists are notoriously thick-skinned.

But what of the opinions of other people? People who met him
in a non-newspaperman capacity. How did they find him? What
did they think of him? Here are a few typical impressions.

Sir Basil Liddell Hart, in many people's eyes the world's
leading military historian, enjoyed a friendship with him that
lasted for ten years. They would often meet over a week-end
drink and have long and stimulating conversations. Connor found
the tall father of tank warfare an absorbing character. Here was a
thinker who had been disregarded and then later proved right so
many times, a true Cassandra. Liddell Hart is a master of strategy
—he can take almost any given situation and analyse it, then
throw in a rational assumption and from it logically produce an
eye-opening conclusion. It is very impressive—and it fascinated
Connor. Liddell Hart often wrote to him commenting on, say,
a given political situation. The gist of the letter would, as often
as not, appear in the form of a Cassandra column. Liddell Hart

Lc

provided, for Connor, a cerebral grindstone. It was used a great deal. In return Connor provided Liddell Hart with an outlet for some of his ideas, ones that needed a bigger, less specialist audience than he might otherwise have got. Like nearly everyone who knew Connor closely, Liddell Hart was interested in the paradox of Connor—the reticent private face behind the rumbustious public façade. He tells of the time when he received a letter from Connor, shortly after their knighthoods had been announced, suggesting that it might be a good idea if they could try to attend the same investiture at Buckingham Palace. 'I think I need a bit of moral support,' wrote Connor, who was a little worried about receiving the accolade. Liddell Hart was very surprised that Connor should have felt in need of aid and replied saying, 'If the two of us got to the Palace together, I'm sure it won't be us that will need the moral support.' In the end, however, because Liddell Hart was in hospital at the time of the investiture, Connor muddled through on his own.

Hammond Innes is one who managed to observe Connor over a reasonable length of time, without getting too embroiled. He was in Italy with Connor on the British Army Newspapers Unit and spent about fifteen months as a member of the same officers' mess. Though he was never a close friend of Connor's—it was difficult to be so when half the other officers were ex-*Daily Mirror* journalists—he nonetheless was able to form a fairly precise attitude towards the man. Innes was rarely party to the fierce arguments that Connor and Hugh Cudlipp indulged in as a major part of their recreation, but he was impressed by the forceful manner in which Connor conducted his case. Innes considered him to be a very able and volatile speaker, relying on the force and brilliance of the words rather than the verisimilitude of the facts. He describes Connor the talker as a 'belligerent poet'. He was initially very surprised at the gentle side of the man. When others would be writing on the progress of the war, Hammond Innes was interested to find that Connor was writing a piece on the effects of that war on the Italians, which might hinge on the sight of a small Italian urchin being offered a piece of chewing gum when what he really needed was a loaf of bread.

An M.P. who was on the receiving end of the thick stick

as much as the bouquet of roses was George Brown. Their relationship was a turbulent one. It couldn't quite be called a great friendship because a man like Connor could never really trust himself to become too close to some public figure whom he might have to criticize the day after he had had lunch with him. This was a great pity for had it developed fully it would have been a notable friendship. As it was, though, they remained on a slightly formal level. They would have lunch together from time to time. They would attend the same parties at the various Labour Party conferences that Connor covered. They found in one another perhaps more than a hint of themselves. Brown is an ebullient man; so was Connor. Brown is fierce in discussion and friendly in discussion; likewise Connor. Their backgrounds were not too dissimilar—both had worked as office boys at the beginning of their working lives. Both had had little more than secondary school education and had made their way through to positions of success and power. Connor liked Brown's forthright honesty—and his fortitude when things were going against him. He respected and admired Brown the Battler. For his part, George Brown had respect for Connor—'There are very few people in a position to help form public opinion to whom I owed as much as I owed Bill.' Considering the great gulf of mutual suspicion that lies between parliament and the press, this last was a more than generous tribute.

These were some of the famous names who were his friends and who knew him well. But what of the others—the men and women who are not household names, the people who lived in the same village as he, the people who caught the same train in the morning to work? In general they are of the same opinion. They found him kind-hearted—and cussed. Outspoken—and reserved. Enigmatic—but they liked him. Nearly all spoke of the fact that he never played the part of the celebrity. They could buy him a beer in a pub—and get one bought for them in return. They could argue with him over a point that arose from a column—but rarely change his mind. They could brag about the relative merits of their cat compared to his. They could give him advice on how to grow bigger sunflowers, advice that was often investigated and occasionally heeded. To those anonymous friends he was 'one of us—not stuck-up at all'. They could relax in his company—but more importantly, he could relax in theirs.

Because he was basically an introvert, Bill Connor's circle of friends was a small one, and a tightly-knit one. But what of the people who did not like or get on with Connor? What of the debit side?

There are certainly plenty of people who did not like him. But the overpowering majority of them simply did not know him. They might read his writings and say that the man talked arrant nonsense—and in their eyes their opinion was correct. There were some who may well have witnessed Connor in fine crushing form, demolishing some innocent with apparent over-brutality. But did they know that this was largely an elaborate display, even part of a private game played by him and his friends? And if the innocent really had been crushed, had had a terrific strip torn off him for his presumption in what he considered an unjust manner, was it really all that undeserved? There are very, very few men in the public eye who can stand the constant idolatry without showing spleen once in a while. Connor was a man who valued his private life highly; it was the thing above all else that made it possible for him to continue the public life and pressures it brought. So if anyone intruded into it at an inopportune moment and asked him for an autograph he was often turned away with a flea in his ear. He suffered fools badly and any man who breaks unheedingly into another man's private world is a fool. He had little if any time for the trappings of fan worship—though he was meticulous in answering every reader's letter. If it were kind he would say 'Thank you'; if it were rude he would return the sentiment in kind and re-doubled.

So there are certainly quite a number of people who experienced a certain amount of verbal manhandling from Connor. That they did not like him is therefore undeniable. They really did not—for the most part—know him, and their dislikes and hatreds are not quite as valid as they might otherwise be. But who else is there who crossed swords with Connor and came away feeling far from friendly? John Gordon for one. This dour Scot is Editor-in-Chief of the *Sunday Express* and he and Connor indulged in a short but acrimonious row in the public print

(Gordon writes a column in the *Sunday Express* every week). It was a skirmish still remembered in Fleet Street, though it happened more than ten years ago in 1958. Connor called it the 'White Feather War'. Gordon had written, in his column, an alleged implication that Connor had, during the war, gone straight from the *Daily Mirror* to 'a cushy job in Naples—and stayed there'. Call a man a coward and you ask for trouble. Call a well-known man a coward—and in the public press—and you are really asking for it. The challenge had been issued. The weapons had been chosen. On 9 April Connor replied:

> I propose to expunge this smear brewed up in the heart of an ungenerous old man whose reputation at its highest is that of a shoddy John Knox. My record is: total service in the British Army, four years, four months . . . my war was largely boring and occasionally risky . . . before the 1939 war I reported the war in Spain, when the Italians were bombing Barcelona. I was detained by the Gestapo at Tempelhof Aerodrome in Berlin in August 1939. After my White Feather War I reported the wars in Malaya, in Singapore and in Korea.
>
> But in all my travels abroad I never saw John Gordon—except once. That was at a cocktail party in San Francisco a couple of years ago. He was doing some fierce hand-to-hand fighting with a dead sardine on toast. A worthy opponent.

Randolph Churchill once spoke of the disadvantages of a famous father. He likened it to living in the shade of a great oak tree. There have been many cases of the children of famous men and women who have found the strain unbearable; often they have grown up bitter and disillusioned. Bill Connor was very aware of this potential danger. It may even have been one of the major reasons he was so adamant about keeping his private life private. One of the things that upset him most about his libel action with Liberace was the effect that it might have had on his children, especially from the point of view of their relationships with schoolmates and friends. He was much relieved to discover that they had not been affected by it—other than a slight increase of youthful pride, a temporary puffing-up of sibling chests.

Perhaps the thing that made it easier for his children was the fact that he wrote under a nom-de-plume. If one was asked one's name it was not immediately seized upon with a cry of 'You must be so-and-so's boy, then.' For every hundred people who knew the name Cassandra, there can have been no more than one who knew William Neil Connor. This protection made life very much easier for all concerned. It was possible vicariously to enjoy the applause without being bathed in the spotlight.

It would be true to say that he was a reasonable success as a father. He was—doubtless due to his own upbringing—a stern man, but fair. The clipped ear when it was received was almost always well-deserved. But the word of encouragement was more in evidence than that of discouragement. At times he could be more reserved towards his family than other fathers. He gave the impression that there were words he wished he could say but something prevented them. But since families have a habit of developing a kind of telepathic communication, his meaning was quickly felt by those concerned. He was aware of the generation gap between parent and child and did his utmost to close it. He was equally painfully aware of the fact that he did not—because of the war—get to know one of his sons until he was four years old. In these days when children are regarded as an automatic by-product of any marriage that is a fairly sobering thought. How many parents are there today who could be separated from the first years of their child's life without undergoing a fairly large degree of emotional strain?

Bill Connor never pushed his children. He had great common sense. He knew instinctively that a child is happiest when it can set its own pace, when it can develop at the speed that suits it. He neither wanted them to follow him into newspapers, nor dissuaded them. He simply presented them with the facts of journalistic life and allowed them to make up their own minds. All the same he probably gave a great sigh of relief when they all decided against it. His attitude was that, if the child decided to follow one particular line of business, he or she should do it properly to the best of their ability. He once said that he did not really mind if one of his children chose to be a burglar 'just so long as he's the best bloody burglar there is'. Children appreciate independence when it it is offered to them on these terms.

Having Bill Connor as a father was an exhilarating experience. He told fascinating and furiously amusing stories of trips he had taken abroad. What were, to other people, household names, were often the people who dropped by at week-ends. Other god-like ones had their clay feet exposed. Still others, who were made out to be villains of the first water, turned out to be exceptionally nice people. Above all Connor instilled in his children a sense of perspective towards the trappings of power and fame; underneath it all, he said, the people who have it are just as human, with the same real fears and joys and weaknesses. Because his interests were so wide and so varied, so were those of his children. He broadened their outlook. They in turn, of course, loved having a famous father—at least, for most of the time.

So there you have it—Bill Connor through the eyes of a number of people. You could love him—or hate him. Or even on rarer occasions feel indifferent towards him. He was outgoing and withdrawn. Quiet and noisy. Kind-hearted and ruthless. Warm and cold. Gentle and rough. Sad and funny. He could growl in a friendly manner—and bite, too. He could be effusive in his greeting—or cut you dead. He had a rapier wit—with the sudden violence of the cosh. He could be a great big teddy-bear— but with claws. He had a tough exterior with a soft centre.

He once wrote, 'O the lovely silly human race, and how I love its crazy smiling face.'

A lot of people felt the same way towards him.

CHAPTER TEN

BEHIND THE MIRROR

FOR a great many years the heroes and heroines of the Horlicks strip cartoon advertisements, that Basil Nicholson had helped originate way back in the early 1930s, expressed their new-found success and satisfaction in the immortal words: (*Thinks*). 'Thanks to Horlicks.'

But life is not like that. It takes more than regular doses of a malty nightcap to mould a successful career. There are a great many other influences, including education and environment. But perhaps the most influential of all are people. They help form and fix beliefs. They act as a measuring rod against which we can compare outselves. They can open our eyes to the world—or shut them tight. We learn most of our scale of values from other people. And the process goes on throughout life. Ideas change because of people. Likes and dislikes also. People are of paramount importance.

In a character as complex and diverse as Bill Connor, it is interesting to see who the people are who influenced him and in what way they affected him. So let us take a look at some of the more interesting and unusual ones.

All his life Bill Connor collected eccentrics, with the same fervour that other men apply to stamps, mistresses and man-hole covers. He was quirky about people who were quirky. He loved the unusual, the flamboyant—even, on occasions, the outright lunatic. He delighted in the exploits of an American named Jim Moran who proved by practical experiment that too many cooks don't spoil the broth, that it is possible to change horses in midstream, that to find a needle in a haystack is child's play if you go about it correctly, and who topped this little lot off by selling a refrigerator to an Eskimo. The fact that Connor had such a high regard for eccentrics was due, no doubt, to his exposure to eccentricity at a very early age. As we have seen, one of his great uncles read the *Financial Times* in a wheel-less hansom cab and collected all the empty bottles of Scotch he had drunk in his cellar.

156

Another relative—his grandfather's brother-in-law—provided him with a further example of unusual behaviour. His name was Ezekiel and his sister kept house for him. Connor loved the story of black comedy that was reputed to have happened after her death.

At the wake held for her, as is the custom in Ireland, all the mourners got very drunk. When the time came to take the coffin down to the churchyard for burial, most of the mourners were too far gone to notice that her corpse was still laid out on the bed. The coffin was duly laid to rest and the oversight was only discovered when Ezekiel returned sorrowfully to the house with a close friend, only to find the corpse still in the upstairs bedroom. The two of them then had to wait until after dark to do their Burke-and-Hare act in reverse. Ezekiel died a few years after with his secret intact; it was only revealed by the friend many years later.

Whether the story is true or not, Ezekiel was certainly one of the more entertaining of Connor's relatives and one whose delightfully odd ways impressed him as a very small boy.

Apart from these two characters and his parents, there was one other relative who had a great influence on Bill Connor. This was his uncle, Frank, who was, like his brother, a Civil Servant. In fact, he was a more successful one than Bill Connor's father and when he retired in 1936 he was Principal Inspector of Establishments in the Inland Revenue. Frank Connor was a very tall man, well over six feet. James Callaghan, the present Home Secretary, who as a young man worked as a clerk in his department, tells a story about him. An enterprising press photographer once took a picture of Frank Connor as he was walking down Whitehall, with Nelson's Column in the background. The angle was such that the column appeared just over Connor's shoulder. The caption, with a reference to his great height, read: 'It will be seen that Nelson's Column is slightly the higher of the two.' Frank Connor's great quality, and the one that left its deepest impression on Bill Connor, was his sense of humour. At his examination by the Royal Commission on the Civil Service in 1929 he was asked: 'What does the Director of Establishments do?' His straight-faced reply, in tones of mock surprise, was: 'Why, he directs establishments.' Douglas Houghton, M.P., who worked closely with Frank

Connor for many years, described Frank Connor's contribution to his part of the Civil Service thus: ' . . . Connor humanized the whole set-up of Establishments. He was a kind-hearted man, who insisted on everything being done in a kind-hearted way. . . .'

Bill Connor was very fond of his uncle. He found in him a gentle critic, someone whom in early years, he could ask for advice. It was advice that he respected and often heeded. In a way Frank Connor was a kind of mentor to Bill Connor. His parents were too close for him to be able to discuss matters with them. Other people or other friends were not close enough or not experienced enough. Over the years Frank Connor watched his nephew's career with ever-growing pride and much encouragement.

When he retired in 1936 Frank Connor returned to his native Northern Ireland to live at Bangor, Co. Down. Being thus geographically removed from his sphere of influence, Bill Connor missed him and his advice and friendship. He therefore sought someone who could take his place, someone he could talk to quickly and easily without having to resort to the telephone or letter writing. He still kept closely in touch with his uncle but he needed someone to act as a good substitute.

Connor found one in William Bliss. Shortly after his marriage in 1938, when Connor and his wife had moved from London to the Chiltern countryside, he met Bliss for the first time. Bliss had been born in 1864, the son of an Oxfordshire vicar, who later became a Catholic and went to Rome to work in the Papal Archives. Bliss had been educated at a private school in Hampstead and later at Stonyhurst. He had turned down the chance to go to university at Oxford and had become a solicitor in London.

Bliss had two great passions—canoeing and writing. He managed to combine them both by writing a number of books about canoeing and the waterways of Britain. He was an extremely literate man, fond of quoting other writers. He also wrote poetry, which he submitted regularly to the *New Statesman* under the pseudonym of 'Yorick'. He and Connor had first met in a local pub and their friendship grew and flowered in the pleasant surroundings of good beer and stimulating conversation. At the time they had met, Bliss had been in his early seventies and was retired, but still very active. Indeed, shortly after Connor had returned from Italy at the end of the war, Bliss took him on a short canoeing holiday on the River Wye. A major part of their friendship was built around long philosophical discussions on writing. They would discuss some small and minutely irrelevant point for hours on end. Connor found Bliss's very orthodox education absorbing. He would talk for hours on why Shakespeare chose a certain word for one of his sonnets. Connor for his part was a professional writer and Bliss, as an amateur, was fascinated by him. During the three years that Connor spent in Italy, Bliss wrote him long letters. They were an extraordinary mixture, always written with great delicacy and a careful choice of words. In the same letter Bliss might talk of the weather, his penchant for gardening, the lack of beer in the pubs and his latest offering to the *New Statesman*. Most of these letters contained a fresh parody or poem that he had written. In one, he writes of his dislike for T. S. Eliot:

> This week I am amusing myself by writing lewd parodies and saying rude things about T. S. Eliot, whose 'nice touch' (my God!) Mr William Whitebait bids us to emulate.
> I dislike Mr Eliot intensely, both as a poet and person. As a poet because he degrades that holy name and as a person because he is a pornographic sniffer and sniggerer. I don't like slinking smut and suggestive sex. Give me Rabelais and let me laugh loud and openly. Mr Whitebait is not likely to print anything I send in. He never does, and anyway, if he admires Eliot, he certainly won't.
> So I send you one of my lewd imitations, a variant of Eliot:
>
>> When lovely woman stoops to folly but
>> Neglects the advice of Mrs Stopes,
>> One thinks the poor girl must have been a mutt
>> And that there won't be quintuplets one hopes.

Bill Connor found William Bliss a very congenial companion, and a useful critic, and he was deeply distressed when Bliss was killed by a car, not long after their canoeing holiday. Connor had a favourite story about this tall, witty and wise old man. Bliss first went to watch the Regatta at Henley back in the 1880s. From that time on he had made it a regular outing, so that by the time he died he had been to no less than sixty-four 'Henleys'. He always, throughout that time, made a point of sitting in exactly the same place by the river's edge. Other regular regatta-goers recognized him and respected his position. No one ever tried to usurp his seat. Strangely, he once claimed not to like rowing. Connor, greatly surprised, asked him why then did he bother to go to the Regatta every year. Bliss's reply was typical: 'I go to watch the trees grow.' In a column he wrote shortly after the death of this 'man with rather cold blue eyes and more conviction about most things than is usually good for people', Connor said: 'Some of us mourn that empty chair.'

It would be foolish to underrate the influence that Bill Connor's father had over him, even though it is a great deal more difficult to pin it down to any one quality or single event. Henry Connor's influence was a profound one, and one that showed up, quite naturally, in Bill Connor's personality, rather than his writings.

Henry Connor was a just man. He had learned justice the hard way—through experiencing injustice. As a young boy he had watched his own father struggle to make a living, which had then been all but taken away by the opening of a rival school and the forced transference of many of his pupils to it. Henry Connor was a gentle man. The inevitability of circumstance, first with the closure of the school and secondly with his inability to pursue a career as a teacher, had made him so. When the gods are so against one, it is often better to bow one's head to fate.

Much of the humanity of Bill Connor's writing is due to his father's influence. So too is the humour. His father was an expert raconteur, and had a very quiet way of telling a joke that made it all the more amusing.

If Henry Connor was responsible for some of the deeper facets of Bill Connor's character, he was also responsible for some of the less deep ones. He was a fanatical gardener. In one letter written to Bill Connor during the war, he described in precise detail exactly what he had planted in his allotment: '. . . three rows of beans, one row of shallots, two rows of leeks, four of beetroot, three of carrots, one of onions, one of peas, a bed of lettuce, two rows of cabbage, and twenty-one rows of potatoes . . .' Connor inherited this great love of gardening, but with one difference. He liked to make things grow, but he had no time for the physical side of the business. He referred to himself as a 'keen, cerebral gardener, who plans the general strategy, leaving the ground tactics to others'.

Bill Connor also inherited from his father a love of music (his father once sang in the special choir of Westminster Abbey), a brass telescope (the 'St Pancras time-keeper'), and a more than passing acquaintance with the incendiary art of bonfires. He told the story thus in 1962:

I have been designing, planning, constructing and maintaining a bonfire.

It has now been burning for eight days and has been described by an eminent bonologist as 'truly one of the finest specimens seen in the Home Counties since they made a bonfire in South London in 1936 that included, among its ingredients, the Crystal Palace.'

I inherited my talent—some would say genius—for bonfires from my father, who said that life without a bonfire wasn't really living at all.

He would get up in the night to attend an important bonfire. In his own words he 'happed it up' and that meant applying more weedy clods to the great steaming mound with a heart of three or four hundredweight of red-hot ashes.

When the bonfire was properly established, which was usually within about forty-eight hours, he loved it to rain, remarking: 'That bonfire is laughing at the rain. Doubt whether any fire brigade could put it out.'

His final seal of approval on his own handiwork was to observe with a mysterious smile: 'Maybe I'll bake some hedgehogs in it. Do 'em in clay, y'know. Finest dish you ever set your teeth into. Never missed it when I was younger.'

There are no hedgehogs in my bonfire.

But there are—or rather were—about half a ton of rotten apple trees; enough hedge clippings to obscure the forest of Dunsinane; more leaves than the Babes in the Wood ever saw; a mound of those horrible cardboard cases that nobody can ever get rid of; a cartload of weeds unfit for compost; four rows of frost-bitten chicory; a quantity of straw, string, old magazines, two pairs of soleless shoes, a broken picture frame and a nice trimming of the dead stalks and leaves of a failed runner-bean crop.

Its plume of smoke and steam, strongly reminiscent of the wisp of smoke and steam that garlanded Vesuvius after the great eruption of 1944, rises vertically into the cold winter air. The Red Indians in the Chiltern Hills are said to be reading smoke-signal messages from it.

I shall probably throw my bonfire open to the public with a small admission fee to go to charity.

It has been a rewarding week.

When Bill Connor's parents first moved down to the Buckinghamshire countryside in the autumn of 1932 it was his first taste of the Chilterns and of the Bucks people who were later to become so much a part of his life. And the first of those was the man who kept the pub next door to the cottage that Connor's parents rented. His name was Frederick Arthur Cutler. He was born in 1889. He loved the countryside with an enthusiasm that soon infected the young Bill Connor. Up to that time his only real contact with places outside London had been holidays spent either in the raw, awesome beauty of the Aberdeen plain or the quiet coastline of Northern Ireland. The Chilterns were something new to him. He explored the great downy pillow of the hills that drops into the flat blanket of the Oxfordshire plain. He watched the beech woods all around go through their chameleon exercise in browns, greys, greens, buffs and russets every autumn. He discovered the Thames Valley—and delighted in his discovery. He found his true home; and Freddie Cutler acted as a guide and friend.

Cutler might have been called, in finest cliché, a salt-of-the-earth type. Perhaps a truer description would be salt of the countryside. He was of medium height and well-built, with a slight stoop, brought on by years of humping barrels and crates. He also had a very individual line in home philosophy. He disliked work, and held that any sensible person should do likewise. He likened work to drink: too much of it and it made you silly. He hated misers. He wanted the Means Tests to be abolished. And he said that on the day it was abolished there should be free beer for all the unemployed—on the Government. He liked Neville Chamberlain—'there's a chap who knows what he's talking about' (this was some six or seven years before Munich). He wanted to found a new penal settlement, which he named Fogies Island, somewhere off the rocky west coast of Scotland. He wanted to round up all the busybodies, killjoys and Mrs Grundys and send them there. And their punishments would be suitably apt. Judges, who asked inanely what a saxophone was, would be made to play that instrument. Bishops who complained about chorus girls would be made to learn to do the splits and the rumba. Temperance people would find that there was nothing to drink on the island except the finest bitter. And the people who inveighed against the vice of gambling would be forced to present the prizes at the national lottery that Cutler wanted to be run. He liked people to be civil and friendly. And he enjoyed sitting round the fire on a winter night with two or three customers just listening to the quiet, and the sound of the old pub sign creaking in the wind.

Cutler was a man of simple tastes and requirements. Connor—who was then deeply involved in the complex and highly competitive world of advertising—found this approach and attitude to life most refreshing. He spent as much of his time as possible, before he finally moved from London, in this atmosphere. And when he began to write for a newspaper, he wrote for men like Cutler, men and women whose wants were little, for ordinary people. Cutler—and others like him—were indirectly responsible for the common-sense approach of the Cassandra column; no phoney frills, no fuss, no pretentiousness—just straight words and sentences with only one meaning.

There are a number of other people who had an influence on Bill Connor to a greater or lesser extent. There was C. O. Stanley, who gave him the chance, albeit in a roundabout fashion, to discover for himself that he could write. There was Basil Nicholson who taught him a great deal about the finer points of cynicism and whiplash invective. When Connor first met Nicholson he was like a boxer with natural ability. Nicholson's influence and biting wit trained that ability, and honed it to a fine cutting edge. Nicholson also showed Connor how the most harebrained of plans can be enjoyable, especially if they are put into effect. Nicholson's vitality had a great deal to do with

Connor's enormous enjoyment of those first exciting days at the *Mirror*, when each day might be the last in the job. And then there was Bart—the man who gave Bill Connor his main chance, who defended him to the hilt when he was under attack, and who taught Connor more about the business of producing a newspaper and being a newspaperman than anyone else. Bart was the first person to realize Connor's talent as a columnist and nurtured it like a delicate flower—though he was often most un-horticultural about it. It was Bart who first led Connor over the commando-course of newspaper life, and who then had the sense to let him get on with it; Bart whose philosophy towards other people was 'let 'em sink or swim'—but who always held a lifebelt behind his back for those he liked.

The other group of people who influenced Connor were, naturally, his readers; or more particularly some of those who wrote to him regularly. There were some who sent in jokes and puns to add to his collection. There was the Egg Man. There was the Collar Scribe. There were a large number of readers who wrote to him from jail. There were begging letters. There were letters from people who thought him to be a kind of ombudsman and tried to enlist his aid to solve their various problems. There was even one woman reader who, in his early days as a columnist, sent him ten-shilling notes without any explanation. There were letters from crackpots and from geniuses. There were countless letters from people wanting to become writers themselves. They were usually great boasting, florid pieces, often starting off 'Dere Sir . . .'. There were friendly letters and abusive ones. There were parcels too. On one occasion, after he had written a piece bemoaning the lack of a good loaf of bread, his office was deluged with hundreds of home-baked loaves from all over the country. On another occasion he had written a column that was highly critical of something or other and was sent a parcel containing human excreta. One way or another, Connor's post-bag kept him in very close touch with his readers and their attitudes.

So far much has been said about Connor the public man and about his major interests. To gain a broader picture of him, it is worth taking a look at some of the minor ones. For instance, there was carpentry. For a great part of his life he was interested in

it. But he did it very badly. The enthusiasm was there; only the
skill was missing. The title that someone gave him of 'The Artful
Bodger' was not lightly bestowed. He had a workshop equipped
with all manner of woodworking tools but the results he obtained
from them were invariably fearsome. And, unlike surgeons who,
as the old saying goes, are able to bury their mistakes, Connor
insisted that his should go on display. He made kitchen stools that
crumpled under the weight of a handful of spilt cornflakes; he
made a dining table (oddly enough, quite successfully) that cost
about three times as much as the most expensive one that money
could buy; he made marble-topped tables that drove holes through
carpets with their legs. He made wind vanes by the dozen. One
in particular was highly memorable. He managed to get hold of
the wooden propeller from a Tiger Moth light aircraft. After
much banging and sweating it was hoisted into position on the
end of a wooden garage. That same night a very strong wind
blew. The propeller, designed to lift a good half ton of aircraft
off the ground, nearly managed to do the same for the garage.
It creaked and groaned ominously all night long. Next day the
wind-vane-to-end-all-wind-vanes was taken down.

Connor was very proud of his lack of talent as a handyman.
He delighted in being so inept with his hands. He boasted about
it through his column:

Am I handy about the house? Leaky taps? Laying lino? De-bung-
ing the bunged-up sink?

I'll say I am. I'm your man.

Did I ever tell you how I changed the needle on the old radiogram
that ended in the ever-intensifying struggle that civilization brings—
The Battle Between Things and Us?

I had in mind buying a new needle for about five bob, but the
salesman winced when I said this and insisted that a super sapphire
job for about twenty-five shillings was the only thing that a percep-
tive, sensitive music-lover like myself would tolerate. 'First class
service for a decade.' he said. 'No mush, no hiss—only the deep
purple of absolute silence.'

I bought it.

I also purchased on the way home a watchmakers' screwdriver to

Mc

slacken the grub screw that holds the needle. It worked perfectly, but the screw fell out and landed, I thought, on the floor.

I couldn't find it. I then searched for it on the carpet with a small table lamp. The shade fell off.

I dropped the lamp, there was a blue flash and all the lights went out. I found the remains of an old candle, and blundered across the hall, tripping up over a chair. The candle snuffed it.

I relit it and plunged into the cupboard under the stairs where a colony of fuse boxes nest together like bats in a barn. Finding the Lost Chord is child's play compared with looking for a burned-out fuse wire under the guttering twilight of one candle power— especially when you stand on brooms that bounce back and bust you over the beano like emaciated Indian students being clubbed by riot police wielding lathis.

Finally I found the burned-out metallic gossamer of what had once been a fuse and reconnected with 5 amp wire where 10 should have been. The lights came on. Back to the carpet. No screw. Heavy breathing followed by a strong ale.

Finally located screw that had gone to earth under the turntable. Tally ho! Tried to dig out with the aid of a ruler. No joy. No screw. Nothing.

Then tilted the whole radiogram to get the screw to roll out. One leg snapped off like a rotten carrot. Lights go off again. Back into the broom cupboard, fighting mad. No spare fuse wire. More blows in the darkness and Indian riot still raging. Reconnect with wedge of silver paper. Lights on again. The Fleet's all lit up. On a radiogram four legs are fine, but three, two or one leg don't help unless the whole ship is listing 45 degrees to starboard.

I snap off the remaining three legs. The madness is upon me. Music box now on an even keel.

No screw but if it's a fight you want I'm your man. Bell sounds for Round Five.

Why not lift the turntable up? It must pull off. Yo-heave-ho. Turntable won't budge.

One final heave and the turntable *does* budge. So do yards of wire entrails and a whole digestive system of condensers and grid-leaks and a shower of volts, amps and ohms.

So you won't play, huh?

Grab hulk of wrecked radiogram and stagger to dustbin. Crash wreckage down on rim. Too large for dustbin so force it down and batter it until it does fit—in instalments.

Heavy breathing again followed by what that snivelling limb of Satan described at the shop as nothing but 'the deep purple of absolute silence'.

Victory for Things. Defeat for Us.

Connor's total inexpertise with materials extended as far as reinforced concrete, home-made variety. He once built a roof for the massive compost heap at the top of his garden. It was made from mighty pine beams covered with sheets of asbestos roofing. It was pivoted at a point one-third of the way from the back edge so that it could be raised up when fresh compost was being dumped into the rotting pit. The trouble was that the whole contraption was so heavy that it needed three very strong men to move it every time. Connor's answer was simple: 'Counterweights! That's what we need.' So he constructed wooden moulds, mixed up the concrete, poured it in and added a massive lattice-work of bent wire to give strength. The whole was allowed to set for three days. At the end of this period three men gathered for the unveiling ceremony—Connor, his brother Mick, and one of his sons. The mould was broken open with all the care and ceremony of a sculptor with his first bronze. Three men stooped, grasped hold of the great concrete pillar firmly and heaved. It crumbled like old soggy biscuits in their hands. Connor was speechless with rage; the other two ran for their lives. He had used gardening lime instead of cement.

Connor also applied his blundering, bull-in-a-china-shop brand of expertise to one of the more neglected arts: cooking *al fresco*. He was a great outdoor cook. But since the weather in this country is usually too bad, he reserved his demonstrations for holidays abroad. His career as a chef of the wide blue yonder started in Italy during the war. He boasted many times of being one of the very few men in history—if not the only one—who had made a forty-eight egg omelette on the side of a mountain near Florence. If pressed he would admit grudgingly that the eggs were not full-size ones, due to the fact that the Italian chickens were having it rough at the time. But it was a forty-eight egg omelette all the same.

Connor was also the inventor of a specially modified Scotch

Broth, again in his capacity as an outdoor cook. Like the monster omelette, the scene was once more an Italian hillside some time in 1944. He had been co-opted by the fellow members of his Mess to build them a soup (he always talked of 'building' soups). He started off with a tin of M. and V.—meat and vegetables (so called) —some diced carrots, dried potato powder, string beans and a can of beetroot. The ingredients were set to boil. When the soup was done it looked and tasted vile, so he set about making certain alterations to it. One by one he removed the ingredients, tasting the remainder each time, and also adding a liberal shot of whisky to take the place of the missing ingredient. Finally there were none of the original ingredients left. It was simply hot Scotch with a thin soupy flavouring. And that, Connor claimed, was how *real* Scotch Broth was born.

Perhaps the longest lived and most celebrated of Bill Connor's manias was of course his cats. He loved them—and had plenty of them to love over the years. His attitude to them is best expressed in the foreword he wrote to his book *Cassandra's Cats* published in 1958:

People either like or dislike cats. You cannot be indifferent to them. Nobody is completely impervious to cats—though cats are often impervious to people. Cat lovers really love cats and cat haters really hate cats.

A few people—a very few—succeed in remaining detached if not neutral about cats, like the old farmer who was once asked if he preferred the society of dogs or cats. He replied: 'Neither. Cats look down on you—disdainful and distant-like. Dogs look up to you and put you on a pedestal where you've no right to be. Give me pigs every time.'

'Why pigs?'

'Pigs? Because pigs is equal.'

I love cats. I like 'em big and small and black and white. I like them smokey-blue and tawny-tabby. I like them when they're young and gay and I like them when they're old and battered. I prefer short-haired cats to long-haired cats—but I still like the long-haired cats.

Cats are the most mysterious animals in creation. The Designer of cats—'what immortal hand or eye?'—began with the idea of creating the most perfect animal of all. It was to be the answer to the rhinoceros, the alligator, the tarantula, the rat, the sting-ray, the cobra, the bat, the barracuda and the vulture.

Sick of terrestrial, aerial and marine horrors, the Designer brooded on the problems of grace and symmetry; of elegance, agility and poise.

So He planned the cat.

There was plenty of time—about a billion years—so the Designer, being the great engineer that He is, went to work on the prototypes and the mock-ups. He built the tiger and the puma, the cheetah and the lynx. He gave them the beauty of speed and power. He bequeathed the gift of silent strength and didn't worry overmuch that they were cunning, cruel, stealthy, ferocious and cowardly. Then He left them in the forests of the night and began work on the Cat.

It was to be small and quiet and neat. Cats don't knock the furniture around or stamp their feet.

It was to be nimble and strong. Cats can jump ten times their own height. Can you jump over the house?

It was to be fleet of foot. If humans were relatively, in proportion to their size, as fast as cats, we would sprint at over three hundred miles an hour.

It was to be able to see in the dark. Cats need no headlights.

It was to be clean. Do you wash ten, twenty, thirty times a day?

It was to be lithe and infinitely flexible. Can you lick the small of your back?

It was to be able to swim without a single lesson, defend itself against dog monsters bigger and heavier by far and find its way home by an uncanny and miraculous instinct that makes modern aerial navigation seem like blind-man's buff.

Remember the cat that walked from Plymouth to its birthplace in Ongar, a distance of 245 miles? Cats perform these prodigious feats time and time again. Across fields, rivers and cities, through rain and storm, by day and by night, cats return to the place whence they came. Footsore, scrawny, famished and often wounded, they arrive back home like thin and terrible ghosts of themselves.

General MacArthur, when he was driven off the island of Bataan, said: 'I will return.' And so he did, amidst panoply and boasting. But ten thousand alley-cats have done the same trick without maps or directions and have settled the job for a bowl of milk and the chance to purr at their own fireside again.

Not only did He give cats the gift of direction but also the gift of affection, of bravery, of fortitude.

Cats gnaw their way out of the steel wires of gins and snares till their teeth are broken and their mouths ripped. They will face any dog in the end and make Custer's Last Stand and The Boy Who Stood On The Burning Deck look like classics of retreat and cowardice. And, strangest of all, they have affection for human beings; kids as well as old ladies; poor as well as rich—even you and me.

But it is a queer sort of affection, as if the Designer suddenly got tired of the excellence of His handiwork and thought that a dash of the old Wickedness and the old Evil would help. The canvas was getting too perfect, so He took a swipe at it with a brushful of tar.

Hence the falseness of cats, the flattery, the thieving and, of course, the cruelty that ends with the young thrush scattered in a pathetic array of blood and feathers in the rose bed and the mouse brought slowly and with infinite care and delicacy to a tortured end. . . .

Bill Connor owned—or as he put it, was owned by—cats for the major part of his life. He wrote about them in his column. Each time a new one came along he boasted that it was even better than the one before. For instance, here is a letter he sent to Mrs Wilson, wife of the Prime Minister.

Dear Mrs Wilson,

The Prime Minister told me at Brighton that your cat Nemo has a psychological chip on his shoulder because he has not been mentioned so far in my column.

I must put this right.

In the meantime, my cat 'Bulgy' Connor sends 'Nemo' Wilson a short treatise on the most beautiful and sagacious animals in the world.

Yours sincerely,

William Connor.

P.S. Betcher a million sardines my cat is better than yours!

He was not quite as anti-dog as he made out. His parents had owned a big Airedale of which he was very fond when they lived at Carshalton Beeches. George Harman, his friend in the country, had at one time a dog that Connor considered to be the finest he had come across, because it would sing Christmas carols in pubs and could climb ladders. But, all the same, cats were his great love.

There is a crude, half-formed theory put forward by some that people can be divided into two categories—cat people and non-cat people. They say that it is the surest guide to a person's temperament. If he likes cats then he has the independence and unpredictability of cats; if he likes dogs, he has the dependence and faithfulness and solidity of those animals. If there is any truth in this theory at all, then Bill Connor was undoubtedly a cat person by temperament. He was independent in thought. He relied on very few people. He could be charming and friendly in the way a cat can be. And he could be totally unpredictable at times. Like a cat, he could—and did—walk out on people. But also, like a cat, he liked the comforts of the hearth.

CHAPTER ELEVEN

'DON'T LET THEM GET THEIR BLOODY HANDS ON IT!'

I N the early part of August 1935 the following appeared in the *Daily Mirror*.

'Dear Sir: This letter is to tell you how much I admire you. I am just a humble working man who has to do any odd jobs that may be going to keep myself and family alive. What you have done is wonderful and lots of people have much to thank you for.

'My wife just presented me with another son and I would like to ask your permission whether I may call him by your name. Please don't refuse this because I think you are a Great Man—Yours obediently, Agha Zenassi.'

*　　　*　　　*

'Sir, I am directed to inform you that there is no objection to your request regarding the naming of your son. I am happy to tell you that a sum of money has been put on one side to assist in your child's education should he come to this country.

'I understand that your Consulate in your city is requiring a commissionaire for the offices. Should you care to take this letter along, I have no doubt that the Consul-General will give special attention to your application.

I am, Sir, yours faithfully, Gustav Wieland, Private Secretary.'

*　　　*　　　*

The admiring Turk got his job.

And the small, bawling, dusky child will have a better chance in life.

But I can see complications ahead for that baby when he grows up. You see, his name is now Adolf Hitler.

The article was headed 'Fairy Godfather' and it was signed 'By Cassandra'. It was the first article that Bill Connor wrote under that name. And, interestingly, it was also the first of many that warned people of the menace of Hitler.

The Cassandra column was without doubt one of the major

phenomena of modern journalism. It ran continuously—apart from a four-year break during the war—from August 1935 to February 1967. It dealt with thousands of topics, from some of historic importance to others of almost total insignificance, and ran to literally millions of words. Bill Connor reckoned that during his career he must have written something over four million words.

And what words. Hugh Cudlipp in his book, *Publish and Be Damned*, a history of the first fifty years of the *Daily Mirror*, said '. . . he [Cassandra] can make his column purr or bark, nuzzle or bite, canter or gallop, soothe or repel'. The column was entirely the work of one man—unlike most other regular newspaper columns—and it was based entirely on the views and opinions of one man. He never claimed that his opinion was the right one; only that it was the one that he held. He said what he thought and in doing so was often voicing aloud the beliefs of the millions of people who were his regular readers. Many of them agreed wholeheartedly with what he wrote. Others disagreed violently. The Cassandra column above all else provoked its readers into taking sides on whatever subject was under discussion.

Right from the start Bill Connor realized that if he was to be an honest journalist he must have absolute freedom. It was for this reason that he never agreed to sign a contract with the *Daily Mirror*. He stayed with them out of loyalty and because he liked them—and because they were extremely fair and gave him the freedom he valued so highly. It was probably the first and last time that any national newspaper has put so much trust in one of its writers.

The column jumped about like an energetic grasshopper from day to day in its subject matter. Every morning it had a new target—or a different view of an old one. It could be deadly serious, as with the warnings against Hitler or the series of articles on drug addiction a year or more before most people had heard of LSD and 'pot'. It could be supremely light-hearted. Indeed, many people preferred Cassandra at his funniest. It could be vitriolic —the word first coined for it by Churchill during the war when the *Daily Mirror* was getting itself into a great deal of trouble over the alleged inefficiencies and inadequacies of the war effort. And it

Nc

could be as soft and innocent as a child. This was particularly evident with articles like the many he wrote about his childhood memories, of miggies and alleys, of liquorice bootlaces and of cars with resounding names like the Arrol-Johnston or Siddley-Deasy. It could be majestic—like the description of Sir Winston Churchill's funeral. And it could be petty. It is said that one can tell a man by the books in his library—if he is lucky enough to possess one. One could say of Bill Connor that you could tell him by the words he wrote.

Regular readers of the Cassandra column took great delight in the old favourites—the old chestnuts the subject matter of which never dimmed and which were given a fresh airing at least once a year. There were perhaps ten or a dozen of them and each in turn would be brought out, aired and re-polished time after time. For instance, there was the Hirsute Practices Act. Connor, all his life, had a distrust of beards and moustaches. He said: '. . . All whiskered people, ranging from bearers of the thin vicious hairline moustache to the face hidden in deep and impenetrable fur are highly suspect. Rightly doubting of their own virtue they pretend to be entirely different parties in order to conceal their own defects.' And so, in February 1957, as a direct result of the beard that the Duke of Edinburgh grew at that time, he drafted and published the Hirsute Practices Act. In it he said that it should be unlawful for 'all male persons above the age of twenty-one to grow hair upon their upper lips, their chins and their chops . . .'. Contravention of this Act should result in the offender being subject 'to a Publick Shaving with cold water and blunt blades'. His bearded and moustachioed readers were outraged and launched into a fierce and good-humoured attack. He replied with a counter-blast in April of that year. A truce was finally called after a particularly effective thrust from some members of an advertising agency. They worked on an electric razor account and sent him a free one as a weapon in his fight. They also sent a group photograph of themselves. Every one of them wore a full W. G. Grace beard. The point was taken.

Another well-loved hardy perennial was the annual dissertation on Christmas Card Warfare. It was sparked off by the hundreds of Christmas cards Connor received every year from all kinds of people from all over the world. And by the hundreds of Christmas cards he sent out each year. He was struck by the thought that a Christmas card—innocent though it looks—is potentially a very offensive weapon. And it can be used in many different ways. For instance, deliberately spelling the recipient's name wrongly is guaranteed to make him feel a little uneasy. Connor rapidly formulated a set of battle rules and they first appeared in his column of 21 December 1953.

He started by saying that more should be known of 'the military postal science of causing Yuletide mortification, annoyance, irritation, inconvenience, vexation, offence, resentment and deep anger'. Rule One in the battle was to know exactly when to send off your Christmas cards. Fire one off too early and you gave your position away. Send it too late and your card tended to be ineffective. It was best to go into action just before the main bulk of cards come thudding through the letter-box. The next important move, he said, was to choose your card for its size. Big important cards can make the recipient feel very unimportant. Expensive Christmas cards can make the recipient feel cheap. And the very small card is downright insulting. 'It shows what you think of the addressee—practically nothing.' The third factor to bear in mind is the content of the card. You have to choose the one that is most ill-suited. So to a teetotal Scots-hater you send a card with a cartoon drawing of a red-nosed man in a kilt. To dog-haters you send cards that are covered with insipid illustrations of lovable lop-eared spaniels. And so on.

A very valuable piece of insult, he said, is to send a perfectly normal looking card with an excruciating inscription inside it. This can either be a rejected verse written by a long-forgotten Victorian maiden lady poetess, or better still a piece of fake Burns. No one will ever know that it was not written by him and recipients will argue endlessly about which poem it was taken from.

The final approach is the one that Connor called the 'Out of season Touch'. The theory behind this is that if you send a card showing a picture of the 'Cutty Sark' in full sail on mountainous seas to someone who has just stuffed himself with 'Christmas pudding, South African Port and crystallized ginger', you will make him feel even more ill. And you will have scored a major tactical strike in the battle.

Every year the solemn lecture on Christmas Card Warfare was repeated. It was a great favourite with the readers. It attracted a lot of willing students. And a lot of Christmas cards.

As we have already seen, Bill Connor was a very keen amateur gardener. But not a very successful one. Grass, apple trees and roses he could manage. With specialist items like asparagus, bonfires and sunflowers he had great success. But when it came to more mundane things like tomatoes and sweet peas, disaster struck. He described it in a column in May 1962.

I have just given immense pleasure to many of my friends. I have brightened their lives. I have let sunshine into dark places.

I was in the tap room of a pub noted for fierce conversations that go on about gardening, and an acquaintance of mine, with whom I have horticultural rivalry, said:

'Growing sweet peas again this year?'

'Yes, I am—I mean, yes I was.'

'Come again?'

'My sweet peas are strictly in the past tense.'

'Frost?'

'No, they're in the greenhouse. Or rather they were in the greenhouse.'

'What happened?'

'I watered them with liquid weed-killer.'

'Pray say that again.'

'I watered them with a can that had contained weed-killer.'

A roar of pure delight shook the pub.

'Intentionally?'

'No, you great dolt.'

'The tomato plants . . . I trust they are well?'

'They are dead, Burned to a frazzle. Withered. Finished.'

Thunderous laughter. Men with dirty great pints in their hands are choking with glee.

'May I enquire into your zinnias?'

'They look as if they have been nursed by a blow-lamp.'

'And how about your dwarf dahlias?'

'Wiped out.'

People are crying with laughter. They are sobbing with glee.

'Your asters? Your sun flowers? Your marrows? Your cinerarias?'
'Scorched. Doomed. Had it.'
Complete strangers come up to me and shake me by the hand
saying:
'Funniest thing I've ever heard of. You've really made my day.
Thanks awfully, old man. You've properly bucked me up.'

It was as a result of this escapade that Philip Zec christened
Connor 'Professor Brown-Fingers', a name in which he took
great—though secret—pride.
A week after the weed-killer episode Connor wrote another of
his many gardening columns. This one concerned a pair of
gardening boots he had just bought. The idea was to do some
digging. . . .

But I hate digging. Last week I set out to do some digging. I put
it off time and time again. I kidded myself that it was going to rain.
I looked at the fork and tried to persuade myself that the tines were
too short. Things became desperate so I laid a trap for myself. It's
rather like playing single-handed draughts against yourself. I went
and bought a pair of gigantic studded and steel-tipped boots that
made ex-Army clod-hoppers look like ballet shoes. They were
obviously built for stamping things to death—like full-sized croco-
diles. They would have made a dinosaur look clumsy in them. I
unloaded these gigantic crushers into the shed and waited. The self-
goading plot ripened. I could not get these boots off my mind. There
they stood, gaping, gawking and yawning at me. You couldn't avoid
seeing them even when you averted your eyes. There they were—
thirty-nine shillings and sixpence worth of accusation. . . . Ultimately
I broke down and put my foot gingerly into one like a bather, testing
the water with his toe. I tried to walk but I felt as if I were in the
stocks. Maybe the boots were nailed to the ground. Perhaps the steel
studs were attracted by some enormously powerful underground
magnet.
But somehow we got moving and a small patch of ground has
been lightly scratched on the surface with deep imprints where the
boots-boots-boots-boots have sunk deep into the cringing soil.

A year later he came across the boots again and was delighted to
be able to report thus:

... from the garden shed came a rumble of thunder and The Boots bellowed: 'Come into the garden, Bill, we're here in the shed alone.'

So I obeyed the order.

But could I get into the great pedestrian containers? Not a chance. They were as rigid as iron. I could just stand on tiptoes on the heel part. The remorseless beetle-crushers were as inflexible as steel ingots. Compared to them the Iron Boot of Grotingen was a ballerina's silken slipper lightly dipped in champagne.

So once again we don't plough the land and we don't scatter the good seed on the ground.

The cerebral gardener had triumphed again.

Connor always had an enormous number of letters from his readers, and many of them were regulars. It was one of these who provided a column every year, the Egg Man. The Egg Man started in 1953. Connor received a smallish parcel in his post one morning. He was a little perturbed about it at first, because he had received quite a number of extremely unpleasant parcels during his career as a journalist. This one looked as though it could have contained a bomb, and so he opened it with great caution. Inside was a beautifully made wooden box. He took off the lid very carefully. There was a note inside which read: 'Dear Cass—the first egg of the season. Remembered that you once wrote that you liked a goose egg for your tea. Hope you will accept and like this one.' The note was unsigned. The egg was a beauty—and much enjoyed. From then on he received a goose egg every year from the Egg Man. It always arrived on time. It was always sent anonymously. This went on for eleven years until suddenly one year no egg arrived. Connor waited a whole year and again no egg came. In 1966 he wrote a sad little requiem entitled 'The Egg Man cometh not'. He was genuinely upset, especially since he had no way of finding out what had happened to his unknown benefactor. All journalists have their regular correspondents. And they have their favourite ones. The Egg Man was one of Bill Connor's favourites. And he was very sad when the one-way traffic ended.

The other regular correspondent of note was the Collar Scribe. He was just as eccentric as the Egg Man, and just as faithful. From time to time—perhaps four or five times a year—he would write a very long, friendly letter to Connor. It was usually a very general letter about nothing in particular, the kind of letter that makes a welcome change from the usual sort that journalists receive, which are either rude or begging or with some axe to grind. What made these letters particularly appealing was the fact that they were written in a very fine carefully formed copper-plate script on both sides of a stiff collar. The Collar Scribe was another whose letters were very well received. He too remained anonymous and he too stopped one day without his identity ever being revealed.

It would be wrong to give the impression that the Cassandra column was amusing all the time. In fact, the reverse is more true. A great deal of it was simply comment on the day's news. Reading back through the columns today is a little difficult without knowing exactly the background to each item. But there were plenty of serious columns that need no explanation. Some of them were great columns. Others not so great—but nonetheless memorable. Perhaps the one above all others singled out for particular praise was that which he wrote after Sir Winston Churchill's death in January 1965.

The last frail petal of one of the great red roses of old England falls. And the sword sleeps in the scabbard.

There is sadness at the going of Winston Spencer Churchill, but there is also exaltation at having lived in the tremendous nine decades of his formidable, famous, above all, happy life.

When Queen Victoria died the grief and the mourning for the old lady was thrown over the nation like a compulsory pall and sadness was almost obligatory. With Sir Winston it is different. To have been alive with him was to have dined at the table of history.

He engaged in and later presided at the two great and most terrible military convulsions in history. World War One and World War Two.

He knew the Kaiser, that ludicrous, preposterous and pathetic figure, and found compassion for him. He acquitted the Emperor Wilhelm of planning the war and offered in his defence the same plea that was raised for Marshal Bazaine when he was brought to trial for the surrender of Metz: 'This is no traitor. Look at him; he is only a blunderer.'

The golden thread of magnanimity was always there from the beginning to the end; from the Boer War to the Hitler War; from bitter defeat at the polls in 1945 to his dying day. When the accountancy of these two cataclysmic struggles is finally balanced out, Churchill is unchallengeable as a leader, for not only did he outlive all his contemporaries in the First World War, he overshadowed all his comrades in the Second World War. Those he has not survived in longevity he has eclipsed in fame and honour. His main adversaries, Hitler and Mussolini, died in squalid ignominy. His political, treacherous and compulsory ally Joseph Stalin was debased, dishonoured and maybe murdered by his own countrymen.

The Fascist and Nazi regimes were swept away. The generals have chattered themselves into obscurity and only President de Gaulle, difficult, intransigent and chauvinistic, remains as a major figure on the European scene.

There is however for the people of Britain a simpler calculation than all the yardsticks of history about the size of the debt we owe this man.

Had he not been there in 1940 this nation of ours would most surely have lost the war and the Nazi hegemony would have ruled Europe to this day. When all was logically lost, he won. Europe was at Hitler's feet, the United States would never have come in had the flame died in England, and Japan would have taken care of all Asia.

When the First World War was over Winston Spencer Churchill asked: 'Is this the end? Is it to be merely a chapter in a cruel and senseless story? Will a new generation in their turn be immolated to square the black accounts of Teuton and Gaul? Will our children bleed and gasp again in devastated lands?

'Or will there spring from the very fires of conflict that reconciliation of the three giant combatants, which would unite their genius and secure to each in safety and freedom a share in rebuilding the glory of Europe?'

We know the terrible answers to these questions and we also know the name of the man who tried so famously a second time to redress the balance of right against wrong.

* * *

With all the grandeur of his deeds and the sonorous rolling sentences that his speech encompassed, there was always the famous impudent colloquial phrase to capture those who were strangers to Macaulay and Gibbon. There was the time which Hitler threatened to wring old England's scrawny neck like that of a chicken. Said the descendant of Marlborough: 'Some chicken, some neck.' And then a few years later when the war was ended, and a well-meaning adviser gently put it to the old man that he should retire at the zenith of his career and not make the error of hanging on too long, Churchill replied: 'I leave when the pub closes.'

Well, the pub has not yet closed but our best and most beloved patron sitting in the chair of St George has gone.'

Few people outside the newspaper business ever realize the cripplingly physical effort involved in writing a regular column. Writing is mistakenly regarded as one of the gentler arts; a popular misconception is that the writer is someone who sits around languidly waiting for inspiration. And when inspiration has finally struck, all the writer has to do is peck furiously at a portable typewriter for a few minutes, rip out the paper and dismiss it with 'Here, print this.' It is quite otherwise. And to appreciate fully the Cassandra columns one must realize what effort was put into each single column. One must know exactly how the column was written.

Bill Connor's normal working day began somewhere around 6.30 in the morning, which was the time he usually got up. He would have breakfast and leave to catch the 8.17 train from High Wycombe to Marylebone. The fifty-minute train journey to London was the first stage in producing a column. During it he would read and absorb totally the six or seven morning newspapers he bought every day. To do this he needed total concentration and demanded complete silence. Many of his fellow travellers made the mistake of trying to start up a conversation with him during the journey; they would be silenced with a baleful stare and a curt request not to interrupt. The thinking and reading process would continue on the bus journey from Marylebone station to his office in the *Daily Mirror*. He usually arrived there at about 9.30. From 9.30 to 11.30 Connor would continue deciding what he was going to write about that day. He would send in a short note to the morning editorial conference saying what his column would be about. He would also do his correspondence—the readers' letters and the business ones. There was a tacit agreement between Connor and his colleagues that he should not be interrupted during this period. It was the period of the conception of the column. At 11.30 he would usually break for a half-hour or so and go for a drink with one or more of his fellow *Mirror* men. Many writers would have taken—and, indeed, do take—an opportunity such as this to discuss with someone else what they were going to write about that day. Connor never did. He was almost superstitious about it. It may also be the reason why the Cassandra column was so highly personal. He never allowed his opinions to be swayed by others at this critical planning stage. He would then return to his office and start to write the column. He would go out for lunch round about 1 o'clock and return to finish off the column by 4.0 p.m. Sometimes, if it was going well, he would be through the writing part by 3.30; at other times it might take him until 5 p.m. to finish. This would be cutting things very fine, since a newspaper starts the mechanical part of production, the setting-up of type and so forth, round about 4.30. One thing that always impressed even the most hard-bitten of the newspapermen was the accuracy of detail in the column. If he said that such-and-such a place was in London, S.E.19, then the sub-editor could rely on it and not have to check it. The other people who found Connor a true professional were the compositors, the men who fit the lines of type into the area allotted. They always regarded him as a 'clean' writer. They knew that his column would always fit into the space allocated to it and that it would need neither cutting nor padding.

By five o'clock in the afternoon the Cassandra column would be in process of setting up in type and Connor was 'available to human beings', as one of his colleagues described it. For a couple of hours he relaxed. Sometimes he would take the chance to have a short nap. Or he might wander round the office talking to friends. Or go across the road from the *Mirror* to one of the many pubs that surround it and are always full of newspapermen. By this part of the day his job was almost done—but not quite. There was still one more thing to be done, and one over which he was most conscientious. He would always walk down to the 'stone'— the printing floor—to collect a proof of his column, to make sure that it was as he wanted it to be. He was a perfectionist in this; the words had to *look* right as well as *read* right. He might put in a comma here, a full-stop there, little touches that were very important to him. He would take the opportunity to have a chat with a printer or a compositor. It was a gesture, and a simple one that was appreciated by the men who are responsible for the mechanical side of the production of the paper. This attention to the smallest detail is one that he shared with perhaps only one other writer on the *Mirror*, Donald Zec. This zeal was not entirely disinterested. Since Connor felt that the column was such a personal affair he did not want anyone else to have a part in it. He once explained it to Zec, thus: 'Don't let them get their bloody hands on it, my boy.' By some time after 9 o'clock in the evening he was ready to go. He rarely got home much before 10 at night. It was a crippling, exhausting way of life and a very far cry from the smoking-jacket and champagne on ice of the fictional journalist. How he kept it up for the thirty-odd years still amazes his friends and colleagues.

EPILOGUE

For a large part of his life Bill Connor had a preoccupation with death. It horrified and fascinated him at the same time. He loathed war, and wrote vehemently against it. He abhorred capital punishment and, along with a great many others, campaigned for its abolishment. He was an agnostic—and yet, during his last couple of years, talked at great length with a friend about the possibility of an after-life.

This interest in death was not always sombre. One of his unlikely friendships was with the obituary editor of *The Times*. A favourite story—which he doubtless told the editor—concerned a friend of his who claimed that he always read the obituary column of *The Times* first thing in the morning while he was still in bed. The friend explained this odd habit by saying that, as long as he didn't read his own name in the column, he knew it was safe for him to get up that morning.

Perhaps as a result of his strange interest, Connor also had a great liking for Famous Last Words. He went so far as to write a column about them:

> I don't know what I shall be saying with my dying breath, but I hope it will be something utterly banal, like William Pitt's farewell. His friends reported that the great man expired saying: 'My Country! Oh, my Country!'
>
> But a more reliable source said that Pitt took off for the-Great-Blue-Yonder remarking cheerfully: 'I think I could eat one of Bellamy's veal pies.'
>
> A certain amount of research on Last Dispatches from the edge of the tomb has been made, but I feel that there has always been a strong tendency on the part of the imminent mourners to tart the script up a bit.
>
> Now comes a useful addition for all anthologists of the final communique. It is a book called *Famous Last Words* by Barnaby Conrad and is published by Doubleday in the United States. It is a splendid mixture of the heroic and the mundane.
>
> On the silver-trumpets-sounding-for-Paradise theme, there is the

famous theologian Isaac Barrow crying: 'I have seen the glories of the world!'

It is offset by the dying English playwright Sir Henry Arthur Jones who, when he was asked whether he would like his niece or his nurse to spend the last night by his bedside, remarked briskly: 'The prettier! Now fight for it!'

There is the tremendous self-satisfaction of the preacher Lyman Beecher quoting St Paul and expiring to this swelling crescendo: 'I have fought a good fight. I have finished my course. I have kept the faith; henceforth there is laid up for me a crown of righteousness which God, the righteous judge, will give at that day. That is my testimony—write it down—that is my testimony.'

Mrs David Garrick, practical to the end, snapped as she accepted her last cup of tea from a servant: 'Put it down, hussy! Do you think I cannot help myself?'

Rupert Brooke, the poet who believed in the relaxed attitude to life—and death—looked up when he was dying of food poisoning and said weakly to his friend Denis Browne: 'Hello!'

Which may be the perfect farewell.

In the same laconic tradition and as a last, last word there is the final brevity from a certain Dr Joseph Green.

His surgeon, who had been urgently called to the bedside, examined his patient, gave his diagnosis and said simply: 'Congestion.' Dr Green then took his own pulse, waited for a second and said equally crisply: 'Stopped.'

He was right—and dead.

True to his interest, Connor himself left some Famous Last Words. The spoken ones were not recorded. But the written ones appeared as the final paragraph of the last Cassandra column to appear on 1 February 1967.

Normal service in this column is temporarily interrupted while I learn to do what any babe can do with ease and what comes naturally to most men of good conscience—sleep easily o'nights. . . .

It was headed, simply: 'Plenty of Time.'

ACKNOWLEDGEMENTS

The publishers wish to thank the *Daily Mirror* for permission to quote extensively from the Cassandra columns. They also acknowledge with thanks permission to quote from the following copyright material:

William Connor, 'The Petrified Suburb', *The Sunday Times*.

Hugh Cudlipp, *At Your Peril*, George Weidenfeld & Nicolson.

Hugh Cudlipp, *Publish and Be Damned*, The Hamlyn Publishing Group Ltd.

William Connor, 'The Going of Him', *New Statesman*.

William Connor, *George Brown*, Pergamon Press, Ltd.